Santa Fe

Photography by Lisl Dennis
Text by Landt Dennis
Design by Jerry Herring

Published by Herring Press

Page 1

The Museum of Fine Arts on Palace Avenue is a stunning
example of Pueblo-style architecture. Opened in 1917,
the museum was designed by I. H. and William Rapp who
were inspired by the mission churches on the Acoma, San
Felipe and Cochiti Pueblos. (Also shown on cover.)

Pages 2–3

This decorative contemporary basket was woven by
Navajo artist Sally Black. The turn of the century Rio
Grande blanket is a collector's item. Both pieces are from
the Dewey Galleries, Ltd.

Page 4

Allan Houser's Offering the Sacred Pipe stands in the
courtyard of the Wheelwright Museum of the American
Indian. The museum exhibits contemporary and historic
works by American Indians from both outside and within
the Southwest. It is the only institution in the United States
housing artifacts and archival material on Navajo religion and culture.

Pages 6–7

The Sangre de Cristo Mountains at the southern end of the
Rocky Mountain chain rise to 13,000 feet and lie to the
North and Northwest of Santa Fe. Frequently, they reflect
a red cast at sunset giving them their name, the Blood of
Christ Mountains.

Pages 8–9

The vintage pickup truck is a ubiquitous Santa Fe symbol.
If it doesn't carry the family dog in the back, pumpkins
will do.

Pages 10–11

An Acoma pot peeking out of a window is surrounded
by authentic adobe made from earth, straw and water.

Pages 12–13

Concha belts are the focal point of the Santa Fe style in
dressing. These contemporary conchas by Navajo artists
Harry Begay and Hosteen Goodluck are from La Bodega.
The Chinle Revival weaving is from John Kania. Both
shops are on Canyon Road.

Pages 14–15

At Las Golondrinas, a Spanish colonial village museum in
La Cienega, the afternoon clouds billow over a descanso, a
spot indicated by crosses where funeral processions
stopped to rest on their way to the cemetery.

Santa Fe

La Villa Real de Santa Fe de San Francisco de Assis is her real name. Everyone knows her as Santa Fe. Salzburg of the Southwest. Sagebrush Shangri-La. The right place. A mecca of mesas and margaritas. High Country spellbinder. The golden city. She's been called a lot of things, mostly good. After all, New Mexico's capital is a lady of a certain age who began to attract settlers before Plymouth was founded.

At a 7,000 foot elevation, Santa Fe maintains a perpetual high. Stretched out on a plain between the Jemez and Sangre de Cristo mountains, she has a year round suntan. Despite winter snow and summer rain, her complexion remains tawny and wrinkled from dryness. Daughter of the earth, she reflects her parentage. Her accessories are green and sparsely festooned. Sweet smelling piñons, firs, and junipers perfume her body and give shaded definition and sensuous softness to her gentle hillocks and enticing cottonwood-lined arroyos. Yellow chamísa, purple asters, lavender lilacs, silvery sagebrush: Santa Fe is also known for the magic of her make-up.

She is among the chosen for "let there be light." Dawn brings the sun's long, laser-sharp rays straight through the stratosphere. Blankets are thrown off, sweaters shed. Bluejays holler hello and owls shut their eyes to the ball of fire which turns platoons of voluptuous overstuffed clouds from pink, to mauve, to gray, and finally to a blinding white as they begin their slow ascending march over the mountains into a soul searing deep blue sky.

An ear splitting thunderstorm. An eye-dazzling display of lightning. A garden-damaging barrage of hail. A tryptich of rainbows. A heart-pounding sunset. Santa Fe puts on a good show. It has produced a fan club of 53,000 residents and 1.3 million visitors a year who applaud her ever-changing performance. She knows what's entertainment and she puts on a good show, day and night.

Mountains turn to blood, valleys turn to gold as the sun welcomes the moon. Bright enough to cause men's shadows to stretch forever on the pinecone-clad forest floors, the moon traverses a star-studded canvas of black velvet and disappears somewhere south of the border.

"I think New Mexico was the greatest experience from the outside world that I have ever had," D.H. Lawrence wrote of his southwestern transformation. "It certainly changed me forever...The moment I saw the brilliant, proud morning shine high over the deserts of Santa Fe, something stood still in my soul, and I started to attend...In the magnificent fierce morning of New Mexico one sprang awake, a new part of the soul woke up suddenly, and the old world gave way to the new."

ANASAZI FIRST CITY INHABITANTS

The settlement of the southwest began with Native Americans. Traces of Anasazi ("Ancient Ones") dwellings dating to 1150-1350 AD are found at Arroyo Negro within the Santa Fe city limits. Ancestors of today's Pueblo Indians who live on nineteen reservations in western and northern New Mexico, the Anasazi had disappeared by the time the Spanish under Francisco Vazquez de Coronado first rode along the banks of the Rio Grande in 1540. Seeking the seven golden cities of Cibola, he found only mud and stone villages.

With a contract from the Spanish crown to colonize the area, Juan de Onate returned in 1598 along with Franciscan friars, soldiers and Indo-Hispanic colonists from Mexico. It was the province's second governor, Don Pedro de Peralta, who established Santa Fe as the capital of Nuevo Mejico in 1610 under orders from Philip III of Spain.

With him, a New Mexican building tradition was born. Peralta set his men to work to construct *El Palacio de Los Governadores,* the Palace of the Governors. Resourceful pioneers, they mixed earth with straw and water, shaped it into building blocks, baked it in the sun, and called it "adobe." It was a process that had been introduced to the Spanish by the Moors.

To this day, many of Santa Fe's buildings, both public and private, especially in the downtown area, are made of, or made to look like, adobe. Many windows are trimmed in turquoise, a color thought to keep the evil spirits away. The majority are flat roofed. Cool in summer, warm in winter, likely to leak in a storm, adobe is charming to look at, expensive to maintain and completely in keeping with the Palace, the oldest government building in continual use in the United States.

The city's first churches, government buildings, Council Chambers, and customs houses haven't survived. Remnants of her early street system have. The result is a nonsensical spider's web of often unpaved, washboard alleys, winding streets, and thoroughfares. Paseo de Peralta, Acequia Madre, Camino del Monte Sol, Galisteo, Alameda: street names evoke the city's past.

By 1680, Spain had held New Mexico for 80 years. But her hold on the area was temporarily interrupted in August when the Pueblo Indians revolted. They killed an estimated 400 Spaniards. Others fled to present day El Paso. The Spanish had withstood the Indian assault in the well fortified Palace of the Governors. What they couldn't withstand was the lack of water. The Indians had diverted an *acequia,* or irrigation ditch, which continues to run through Santa Fe to this day.

With the Spanish gone, some of the revolting Indians moved into the Palace where they practiced their religion, rather than the white man's. It took the Spanish 12 years to regroup. In 1692, Spanish nobleman Don Diego De Vargas recaptured the city. Many of the old families returned with him as well as numerous new colonists, many of whose descendants remain in Santa Fe to this day.

With roughly 64 per cent of the city's population of Hispanic origin, Hispanic names such as Baca, Roybal, Padilla, Chavez, Archuleta, Lucero, Martinez, and Garcia far outnumber the Browns and Joneses in the Santa Fe telephone book. Nevertheless, Anglo newcomers are coming into town at a far greater clip than would ever have been anticipated. In the 1979 Santa Fe telephone book, Martinez outnumbered Smith 419 to 54. But in the 1985 book, the Smiths were gaining. It was Martinez 449, Smith 128!

Today, several Santa Fe families, including the prominent Ortiz y Piños family, can trace their ancestors' arrival in the capital back to the late 17th century. When Nicolas Ortiz and his wife Doña Maria Coronado moved to Santa Fe in 1693, they became the first generation of what 300 years later would be a family with 15 generations

of hard-working New Mexicans with cultural roots passing through Mexico City back over the Atlantic to Spain.

The year 1821 marked the freedom of Mexico from Spanish rule. Until that time, outsiders, especially merchants, were personae non grata. In fact, Lt. Zebulon Pike, of Pike's Peak fame, had been arrested in 1807 for trespassing over the border.

CAMINO REAL AND SANTA FE TRAIL
COMMERCIAL HIGHWAYS TO OUTSIDE WORLD

Mexico, however, wasn't anywhere near as border conscious. She welcomed outside commerce. The Camino Real from Mexico City to Santa Fe, through Chihuahua and Albuquerque, had long been an artery of commerce with Santa Fe. It was especially busy the quarter of a century following Mexican independence. Mexican silver was the main eye dazzler, producing a remarkably stabilizing effect on the monetary system of the United States. Hundreds of thousands of dollars of Mexican silver in specie and bullion were carried by mule teams and patiently and painfully dragged by ox carts to Santa Fe.

By the close of 1824, the Mexican peso had reached Missouri in such numbers and was circulating so freely that it was accepted by the federal land office in Franklin at par weight with the American dollar.

The primary cause behind this free flow of dollars and pesos was that the famed Santa Fe Trail had been opened up in 1821 by William Becknell. A trader, Becknell had seen that fortunes would be made by Mexico's change of heart. Anxious to be the first to cash in on the rewards, he set out in 1821 along old Indian trails and those made by other mountain men with a string of pack mules loaded with dry goods from Franklin, Missouri, 100 miles east of Independence. It would become the starting point for later wagon trains.

Fighting the elements and the Indians in his historical groundbreaking trek West, "from civilization to sundown," Becknell sighed with relief when he broke free of the mountains and emerged onto the gentle North Eastern New Mexico plains that stretched southward to the first settlements.

A troop of uniformed Mexican soldiers rode out to meet him near current-day Las Vegas, New

Mexico. Despite the language, Becknell understood enough Spanish to realize that all Santa Fe was waiting in the Plaza to buy whatever he had for sale. There was no question about the fact that he and his goods were welcome.

The next year Becknell rode back with other followers, this time with three white-topped freight wagons, the first ones to travel the southern plains.

After word had spread across the U.S. that this trip had been even more profitable than the first, the movement back and forth along the Santa Fe Trail steadily increased. There was money to be made and early adventurers wanted a part of the action.

Stories about the prevalent Mexican forms of amusement—cockfights, rodeos and *fandangos* (dances)—whetted men's appetites. And caused them to set out on an adventure which made many an early merchant's cup to run over. Townfolk turned out en masse to welcome the dust-begrimed teamsters who were required to pay heavy custom duties on each wagonload regardless of the intrinsic value of the goods: sugar or silk, velvet or pelts.

Among the Americans who cast their fortunes and made their fortunes on the Santa Fe Trail were Meredith M. Marmaduke who later became governor of Missouri, Phillip Thompson who learned to speak Spanish better than English, and Josiah Gregg whose book, *Commerce of the Prairies,* is the standard reference of early trail life. These men and many others helped to carve the parallel ruts of endless wagon wheels whose deep wounds continue to dissect the wind-blown plateaus of northwestern New Mexico to this day.

Many of the towns along the old Santa Fe Trail are still there. Passing through Malta Bend, Fort Osage, The Narrows, 110 Mile Creek, Lost Spring, Turkey Creek, Buffalo Bill's Well, Fort Zarah, Cimarron Crossing, La Jornada, Rabbit Ears, Wagon Mound, La Junta, San Miguel del Vado, Pecos Pueblo, Glorieta Pass, Rock Corral, the trail ended at the Plaza de Santa Fe.

It was not everyone's idea of the pot of gold at the end of the rainbow. Not everyone was impressed with what they found at the end of the trail. Certainly not the author of a description of Santa Fe which appeared in the 1830s in a leading New York newspaper.

"To dignify such a collection of mud hovels with the name of 'City,' would be a keen irony; not the greater, however, than is the name with which its Padres have baptized it," the early journalist wrote. "To call a place with its moral character, a very Sodom in iniquity, 'Holy Faith,' is scarcely a venial sin; it deserves Purgatory at least. Its health is the best in the country, which is the first, second, and third recommendation of New Mexico by its greatest admirers. It is a small town of about two thousand inhabitants, crowded up against the mountains, at the end of a valley through which runs a mountain stream of the same tributary to the Rio Grande. It has a public square in the centre, a Palace and an Alameda; as all Spanish Roman Catholic towns have. It is true its Plaza, or Public Square, is unfenced and uncared for, without trees or grass. The Palace is nothing more than the biggest mud-house in the town, and the churches, too, are unsightly piles of the same material…Yet they have in Santa Fe all the parts and parcels of a regal city and a Bishopric.

"The Bishop has a palace also; the only two-storied shingle-roofed house in the place," the journalist continued disparagingly. "There is one public house set apart for eating, drinking, and gambling; for be it known that gambling is here authorized by law. Hence it is as respectable to keep a gambling house, as it is to sell rum in New Jersey; it is a lawful business, and being lawful, and consequently respectable and a man's right, why should not men gamble?

"And gamble they do. The Generals and the Colonels and the Majors and the Captains gamble. The judges and the lawyers and the doctors and the priests gamble, and there are gentlemen gamblers by profession! You will see squads of poor peons daily, men and women and boys, sitting on the ground around a deck of cards in the Public Square, gambling for the smallest stakes," the reporter's opinioned diatribe continued.

"The stores of the town generally front on the Public Square. Of these there are a dozen, more or less, of respectable size, and most of them are kept by others than Mexicans. The business of the place is considerable, many of the merchants here being wholesale dealers for the vast territory tributary. It is supposed that about $750,000 worth of goods will be brought to this place this year, and there may be $250,000 worth imported directly from the United States.

"Yet, although dirty and unkempt, and swarming with hungry dogs, (Santa Fe) has the charm of foreign flavor, and like San Antonio retains some portion of the grace which long lingered about it, if indeed it ever forsakes the spot where Spain held rule for centuries, and the soft syllables of the Spanish language are yet heard."

Fifteen years later in 1846 after Santa Fe had been captured by the U.S. Army, Lt. W.H. Emory wrote further about the town. "The houses are mud brick…, generally of one story. They are forbidding in appearance from the outside, but nothing can exceed the comfort and convenience of the interior. The thick walls make them cool in summer and warm in winter," he wrote of his military reconnaissance from Fort Leavenworth, Kansas to San Diego, California through Santa Fe. "The better class of people are provided with excellent beds, but the poorer class sleep on untanned skins. The women here…appear to be much before the men in refinements, intelligence, and knowledge of the useful arts. The higher class dress like the American women, except, instead of a bonnet, they wear a scarf over their head, called a *rebozo*. This they wear asleep or awake, in the house or abroad. The dress of the lower class of women is a simple petticoat, with arms and shoulders bare, except what may chance to be covered by the *rebozo*.

"The city is dependent on the distant hills for wood, and at all hours of the day may be seen jackasses passing laden with wood, which is sold at two bits, twenty-five cents, the load. These are the most diminutive animals, and usually mounted from behind, after the fashion of leap-frog. The jackass is the only animal that can be subsisted in this barren neighbourhood without great expense…"

Among the legendary pioneers to ride the Santa Fe Trail was the widow Eliza Sloan. The Spanish Trail having opened up from Santa Fe to the California gold fields, she was en route to the West Coast when her purse with all her money was stolen in Santa Fe. An enterprising lady, she sold a piece of gold jewelry, started a boarding house and promptly prospered.

Within two years, she had made enough money to sell her business and climb aboard a wagon again. This time, she didn't continue to California but returned to Missouri. She and her two children were to return frequently to Santa Fe, how-ever. A dozen times to be exact. "My mother had become a real trail nomad. Thereafter, she was never happier than when passing over the road to Santa Fe," Marian Sloan Russell recalled in the mid-1930s. Then in her 90s, she had returned to Santa Fe to be greeted as the oldest living pioneer to have traveled the Santa Fe Trail.

LAMY, LEGENDARY PIONEER AND ARCHBISHOP

I t was at that time Marion Sloan Russell recalled walking hand in hand as a small girl around the Plaza with Kit Carson and being placed in the newly established school started by Archbishop Jean Baptiste Lamy.

Perhaps no one in the history of Santa Fe has been more talked about and written about than this remarkable Frenchman. Born in the Auvergne, he came to America as a young mis-sionary in Kentucky. Recognized by the Vatican for his zealous devotion to the church and strong administrative skills, he was consecrated as Bishop in November 1850.

Sailing from New Orleans through the Gulf of Mexico, he was shipwrecked. All his vestments, books and a "fine wagon for the trip over the plains to Santa Fe" went down with the ship. Undaunted, Lamy made it to San Antonio, then by army train to El Paso and finally by horseback up the Rio Grande.

The townspeople along the way turned out in droves to welcome their newly appointed good shepherd. But not the priests. "They do not want the bishop," wrote Father Macheboeuf, Lamy's vicar general. "They dread a reform in their mor-als, or a change in their selfish relation with their parishioners."

On August 6, 1851, Lamy was met by a proces-sion from Santa Fe which had come out to meet him. According to Pulitzer Prize-winning histo-rian Paul Horgan, "the weather was hot and dry. There had been an extended drought. He entered the city amid crowds of citizens and accompa-nied by 8,000 Catholic Indians who animated the triumph with sham battles and dances. The can-non of Fort Marcy fired salutes. A *Te Deum* was sung in the parish church of Saint Francis. A state dinner followed at the house of the resident vicar, Father Ortiz. The day was crowned by a good omen: rain fell in torrents. Everything indicated a good beginning for the bishop."

Establishing a primary school in which English was taught in Santa Fe for the first time, a con-vent school for girls and a college for young men, the ambitious young cleric was determined to run the church his way. His priests either reformed, departed or were excommunicated.

A man of God as comfortable holding a chal-ice as a pair of reins, Lamy was a unique blend of frontiersman and spiritual leader. He was devoted to his flock. He rode for days, weeks, months, in order to hear their confessions, say mass and shore up the foundations of the church. He once rode 3,000 miles over a period of six months to visit his parishioners. Another time, he and a party of twenty-five, including nuns, brothers and priests, successfully held off a party of 300 Comanches.

He also saw the fruits of his labor. Churches under his jurisdiction grew to 135, the number of priests to 41. He inaugurated Santa Fe's first hospital and orphanage.

Of all Lamy's material accomplishments, the Midi-Romanesque style cathedral of St. Francis, built by stone masons from France and Italy, is the best known and continues to dominate the Santa Fe skyline. Its two steeples mercilessly uncompleted, its hard lines and stone walls joltingly incongruous against an almost uninterrupted neighborhood of mission- and pueblo-style adobe architecture, the building is a testimony to Lamy's lack of sympathy for Southwestern Hispanic tradition and his dogged determination to bring the New Mexican church into conformity with the rest of the U.S.

Thinly disguised but immortalized nevertheless by Willa Cather in *Death Comes for the Archbishop*, Lamy is the hero in what many consider the author's finest novel. She wrote in a letter, "the longer I stayed in the Southwest, the more I felt that the story of the Catholic Church was the most interesting of all its stories. The old mission churches…had a moving reality about them; the handcarved beams and joists, the utterly unconventional frescoes, the countless fanciful figures of the saints, no two of them alike, seemed a direct expression of some very real and lively human feeling."

Her own attachment for Santa Fe and New Mexico are seen through her description of the Archbishop's early morning realization. Wrote Cather, "In New Mexico, he (the Archbishop) always awoke a young man; not until he rose and began to shave did he realize he was growing older. His first consciousness was a sense of the light dry wind blowing in through the windows, with the fragrance of hot sun and sagebrush and sweet clover; a wind that made one's body feel light and one's heart cry 'Today, today,' like a child's."

Lamy's final years in Santa Fe are gently described in the final chapter of her novel. "This period of reflection the Archbishop spent on his little country estate, some four miles north of Santa Fe. Long before his retirement from the cares of his diocese,…(he) bought these few acres in the red sandhills near the Tesuque pueblo, and set out an orchard which would be bearing when the time came for him to rest. He chose this place in the red hills spotted with juniper against the advice of his friends, because he believed it to be admirably suited for the growing of fruit…

"Some years afterwards, he built a little adobe house, with a chapel, high up on the hillside overlooking the orchard. Thither he used to go for rest and at seasons of special devotion."

The little chapel, now a part of a quiet resort called the Bishop's Lodge, is just as the Archbishop left it. With its pitched roof and painted glass windows, it is a frontiersman's simulation of a rural French *eglise*.

"MANIFEST DESTINY" UNITED NEW MEXICO TO U.S.

In the middle of the 19th century, Santa Fe was a crossroads of the Southwest. By 1846, in fact, the doctrine of "manifest destiny" necessitated New Mexico's becoming a part of the United States. War was declared against Mexico and Brigadier-General Stephen Watts Kearny was sent to lead his "Army of the West" from Leavenworth, Kansas via Bent's Fort on the Arkansas River through New Mexico to California.

James Magoffin, a trader on the Independence-Santa Fe-Chihuahua Trail, was sent to Santa Fe with a dozen of Kearny's men. Married to Doña Maria Gertrudes Valdez de Beremende, a cousin of Manuel Armijo, Magoffin was to handle the negotiations for the American take-over. He was sufficiently persuasive, some feel through bribery, that when Kearny and his troops approached Apache Canyon to the east of Santa Fe, the Governor and his Mexican troops fled.

On August 18, 1846, the acting governor, Juan Bautista Vigil y Alarid surrendered and the American flag was hoisted over the Palace of the Governors. A bard in the company put it succinctly when he wrote,

"Oh, what a joy to fight the dons
And wallop fat Armijo!
So clear the way to Santa Fe,
With that we all agree, O!

Rather than sack the town, Kearny wisely left well enough alone. The settlement of the Southwest was important to the U.S. government and nothing must prevent Santa Fe's continuing attraction to enterprising settlers.

One of the ways to improve the city's appearance was to launch a beautification of the Plaza. A bandstand capable of seating 15 musicians was built and recitals were held every night. Wagon trains could continue to unload their goods on the Plaza, but they couldn't camp there. Butchers could no longer slaughter on the Plaza nor hang their meat there. Anyone found drunk on the Plaza would be jailed. Flowers were planted. Walkways built. And street cleaners hired to pick up after man and beast.

Santa Fe was becoming civilized.

Meanwhile, some of the Hispanic population in the newly conquered New Mexico felt betrayed by their leaders and began to plot the overthrow of the *gringo* usurpers. They might have been successful if Doña Tules, one of Santa Fe's *grandes dames,* hadn't overheard one of her servants talking about the scheme. Owner of one of the town's gambling halls, she was portrayed by Harper's Monthly Magazine in the shocking act of smoking a cigarillo. A friend of the free-spending American troops who undoubtedly helped the lady to have ample funds to indulge her habits, Tules passed along her knowledge of the upcoming insurrection to the American commanding officer.

The Santa Fe plotters were arrested, briefly jailed and in some cases went on to become important in the New Mexican territorial legislature. Several, in fact, including Nicolas Piño, joined a militia company formed in January 1847 to march north from Santa Fe to quell an Indian insurrection in Taos in which New Mexico's first U.S. Governor, Charles Bent, was murdered along with several other prominent Anglo-Americans.

Another military victory in 1862 by the now fully-entrenched U.S. forces (Union) allowed the territory to continue to grow in importance. In early 1862, Confederate forces invaded New Mexico. Brigadier General Henry H. Sibley, a former U.S. officer who had been stationed in New Mexico, was authorized to conquer the territory, probably in an effort to make the Confederacy a sea-to-sea power from Virginia to California.

After a brief fight with Union troops at Fort Craig, Sibley continued his march to Santa Fe, but the battle of Glorieta Pass near the capital was the turning point. The Confederate supply train was destroyed and Sibley was forced to beat a retreat.

THE INFAMOUS SANTA FE RING

No sooner had the smoke cleared from this confrontation than different but no less dangerous battle lines began to take shape. In the years following the Civil War, the Territory of New Mexico was dominated by a group of men, sometimes called "The Santa Fe Ring," whose position allowed them to influence the economic, political, legal, and administrative system of the territory. Later on, secret societies like *Los Gorros Blancos* ("The White Hats") and *Los Caballeros de Ley y Orden* ("The Knights of Law and Order") were formed to stop the Ring from stealing from the townspeople. But infighting among the Hispanics was so prevalent that the groups could do nothing. According to historian Richard Maxwell, Santa Fe at the turn of the century was "the only place in America where assassination became an integral part of the political system."

Under the leadership of Thomas B. Catron, who had been territorial general before joining forces with Stephen Benton Elkins to form the law firm of Elkins and Catron, the Santa Fe Ring included merchants, lawyers, judges and politicos, most of whom were Republicans. With their fingers in every pie—business, railroads, ranching, and mining—the Ring's biggest "business," or one could say Santa Fe's biggest business, was in stretching the borders of land grants.

Until 1854 when the government in Washington appointed a surveyor general for New Mexico, title and boundaries to all territorial land was less than clear. Holdings were complicated by centuries of varying grant authorship, including the King of Spain, the Republic of Mexico, and the provincial governor. Land could be given to a community for grazing purposes; to an individual for some outstanding service, such as settling an area or defense against Indians; or to an Indian pueblo.

One of the most controversial grants Northeast of Santa Fe near the Colorado border belonged to Lucien B. Maxwell. It was a 97,000 acre spread that was to grow through endless resurveying by the right people with political clout to a staggering 2,000,000 acres.

When the first U.S. Surveyor General William Pelham arrived in the capital of New Mexico in 1854, over 1,000 claims waited settlement, of which 197 involved large private grants. The Ring was, of course, more than willing to help out. Its members were especially interested in the Beaubien-Miranda claim.

Acquired by Maxwell, and subsequently known as the Maxwell Land Grant, the holdings had suddenly become enormously valuable. Gold had been discovered on the land. Maxwell was anxious to sell out and asked for a new government survey which presented him with rightful ownership to 22 leagues, or 97,000 acres.

The sale went through. Maxwell became richer by $1,350,000 and a syndicate which included the Santa Fe Ring's omnipresent Catron and Elkins renamed its new holdings the Maxwell Land Grant and Railroad Company. At the same time, they hired W.W. Griffin, U.S. Deputy Surveyor of New Mexico, to survey the land again.

Amazingly enough, the gentlemen's spread had somehow grown in size. Griffin said the borders of the Maxwell Land Grant encompassed two million acres, not the paltry 97,000 acres which Congress and the Secretary of the Interior had granted him in 1869.

Through an endless series of lobbying campaigns in Washington, knowing the right judges and lawyers, gaining the editorial support of the Santa Fe *New Mexican* newspaper and, of course, ample money with which to grease the wheels of the deal, the Maxwell Land Grant was able to make its two million acres stick.

At the time of the zenith of Maxwell's wealth and influence, he reigned over a feudal fiefdom that no French baron of the 14th century could have outshone. A remarkably amiable, fair man, Maxwell employed over 500 workers who helped him raise cattle, sheep and grain which he sold to the quartermaster and commissary department of the U.S. Army in the military district of New Mexico.

His house was enormous and always full of guests. Colonel Henry Inman, assistant quartermaster, U.S. Army, on the Santa Fe Trail, frequently spent the night there. "I have slept on its hardwood floors, rolled up in my blanket, with the mighty men of the Ute nation lying heads and points all around me, as close as they could possibly crowd, after a day's fatiguing hunt in the mountains," he wrote. "I have sat there in the long winter evenings when the great room was lighted only by the cheerful blaze of the crackling logs roaring up the huge throats of its two fireplaces built diagonally across opposite corners, watching Maxwell, Kit Carson, and half a dozen chiefs silently interchange ideas in wonderful sign language, until the glimmer of Aurora announced the advent of another day. But not a sound had been uttered during the protracted hours, save an occasional grunt of satisfaction on the part of the Indians, or when we white men exchanged a sentence."

A prince among landowners, Maxwell continually entertained, dazzling visitors by his solid silver table service. He wasn't one to forego the pleasures of his wealth, evidenced in what was frequently as much as $30,000 in gold, silver, greenbacks, and government checks which would be tossed all together into an unlocked dresser along with his long johns. He was unconcerned over theft: "God help the man who attempts to rob me and I know him!" he told a friend.

As Maxwell's holdings grew, the Santa Fe Ring became more powerful than ever. From the late 1860s until 1885, nearly every governor, as well as countless other federal officers, appeared to be a member of this elite men's club.

The rewards of being a member made the membership fee of small consequence. After all, land was really the only important medium of currency in New Mexico and the entire West at that time. And until mining, ranching and railroading took over the interests of the Ring, its main concern continued to be "settling" land grants—always to its own benefit and the benefit of the "friends" of the Ring, of course.

When George W. Julian took over the surveyor general's job in 1885, he discovered that the Canada Ancha grant, originally 130 acres, was up to 375 square miles, while the Cañon de Chama grant of 184,000 acres had shot up to 472,000 acres.

Most of the lawyers in Santa Fe took their fees in land. The result was that eventually over 80 per cent of the original Spanish and Mexican land grants went to their fellow Americans or to themselves. Going on to become mayor of Santa Fe and then first U.S. Senator from the state, Thomas B. Catron was always one to come out on top. In the late 19th century, he was, in fact, the largest land owner in New Mexico. In 1894, it was reported by *The New Mexican* that he had an interest in 75 grants, owned nearly two million acres, and was part owner or attorney for four million more. A year earlier, Catron had gone on record to declare that his holdings included:

8,000 acres in patented homesteads
15,000 acres of the Baca Grant
50,000 acres of the Mora Grant
11,000 acres of the Gabaldon Grant
80,000 acres of the Beck Grant
24,000 acres of the Piedra Lumbre Grant
7,600 acres of the Juana Lopez Grant
2/3 of the 78,000 acres of the Espirito
   Santo Grant
1/2 of the 21,500 acres of the Tecolote Grant

Remarking sarcastically that "the office of governor required no more than to count sheep and people to report to Washington," Governor Lew Wallace pretty much summarized the affairs of New Mexico until the beginning of the 20th century.

By then the Atchison, Topeka & Santa Fe Railway was crossing the state, bypassing the capital because the hills below Santa Fe presented difficult engineering problems. The return on such an investment didn't warrant the expense, the company insisted.

Once again, Archbishop Lamy came to the rescue. The power behind a $150,000 bond issue to build a branch line to connect Santa Fe with the main line, he was rewarded when the junction where the two lines met was named after him. The branch line was used primarily for freight, although passengers were also transported. Today, Santa Fe has no direct passenger train service once again. Passengers headed for Santa Fe must be met at the depot in Lamy, New Mexico, and be driven the spectacular 17 miles through the sagebrush, through the piñon, through the junipers into what has become known as Santa Fe, The City Different.

NEW MEXICO BECOMES 47TH STATE

Becoming the 47th state on January 6, 1912, New Mexico soon discovered that by capitalizing on its unique architecture, tri-cultural population, and phenomenal scenery, it could attract outsiders. Word would have to be gotten out, however, that there was something worthwhile to be seen in New Mexico.

As William W.H. Davis, former U.S. District Attorney for the territory had written as early as 1857, "There is no country protected by our flag and subject to our laws so little known to the people of the United States as the territory of New Mexico. Its very position precludes an intimate intercourse with other sections of the Union, and serves to lock up a knowledge of the country within its own limits. The natural features differ widely from the rest of the Union, and the inhabitants, with manners and customs of their Moorish and Castilian ancestors, are both new and strange to our people. For these reasons, reliable information of this hitherto almost unknown region can not fail to be interesting to the public."

"Magical" is the adjective frequently used to describe New Mexican landscapes. "Enchanting" has long served visitors anxious to tell friends about Santa Fe. Magic and enchantment are reasons enough to draw strangers to this particular corner of the southwest.

But was there something more which drew the faithful to Santa Fe? "It was always difficult to fix upon the particular stimulus amid all the general charms which had most to do with bringing modern colonists to town," Paul Horgan wrote in *The Centuries of Santa Fe.* "Yet beyond these general charms something else could be felt. It was the insinuation of freedom of behavior, not in any publicly unsavory terms, but rather in an opportunity for an individual man or woman to live a life of free expression. In modern times, was this the most significant—and perhaps the most Latin—of attractions about Santa Fe?"

An advertisement in the *New Mexican Review* of April 12, 1900, offered another reason to come to New Mexico. No place else on the continent was better suited for the traveler to "find rest from the daily monotony of an active life and recuperate his gray matter," it said. "It is an ideal spot for a summer's outing, and will compare favorably with a trip to Egypt, while not taking up so much time and being less expensive."

"LUNGERS" DRAWN BY HIGH ALTITUDES

Many newcomers to New Mexico came for their health. "Lungers" were drawn to Santa Fe's high altitude and pure air in an effort to overcome their various ailments, tuberculosis in particular.

Under the direction of Dr. Frank Miera, Sunmount Sanitarium, started in 1903, was the temporary address for what would become some of Santa Fe's most prominent early citizens near the turn of the century. Promoted as a health resort and to help minimize the concern many felt about "TB," the institution was flawlessly run.

White wicker furniture, Indian rugs, excellent food and air—lots of air, night and day—were all part of the ambiance and regime at Sunmount.

It was also nurturing ground for some of Santa Fe's early 19th century talent. Rather than to become part of the Lost Generation on the Left Bank or swallowed up in the melting pot of Greenwich Village, the town's art colony set to work to build the pond in which its members would become big fish. With the establishment in 1909 of the Museum of New Mexico, Santa Fe was on the threshold of being discovered. "Thespian groups produced small plays for festive occasions; the poetic minded gathered for tea in cottages and enjoyed and criticized each other's verses. And local artists of some renown held classes on the grounds," recalled Wayne Mauzy, a patient at Sunmount.

Famed architect, John Gaw Meem, responsible for introducing the architecture to become known as "Santa Fe Style," and artist William Penhallow Henderson and his wife, author and poet Alice Corbin Henderson, were first introduced to Santa Fe through their stay at Sunmount. Like many others, they were transplanted Easterners. Indeed it was Alice Corbin who asked poets Carl Sandburg and Vachel Lindsay who were visiting Santa Fe to read their work to the patients.

Once cured, the Hendersons and Meem, like so many other former Sunmount patients, stayed in Santa Fe, adding to the city's rich cultural life.

Poet Witter Bynner was another. Arriving at Sunmount in 1922 to visit Alice Corbin Henderson, he recalled that, "It troubled me at first to stay in a building which was half hotel, half sanitorium for tuberculars. But I was soon persuaded that I was safer at Sunmount than in a New York trolley car…"

Bynner was to remain in Santa Fe the rest of his life, writing and receiving visitors from throughout the world. In 1980, his poems would, in fact, become the springboard for composer Ned Rorem's "The Santa Fe Songs" commissioned by the Santa Fe Chamber Music Festival.

"The Southwestern landscape, more than any other in North America, reduces vainglory in a man and enforces his exact, or at least his reasonable, importance…If he but brings water, the desert will bloom," Bynner wrote of his new environment. Cosmopolitan, debonair, witty and dedicated to the art of living, Bynner like so many early Santa Feans, delighted in the integrity of his own house's adobe exterior with its voluptuous curves and melted edges. He also delighted in the opportunity to transform its interior into a sophisticated and eclectic blend of the finest Southwestern and European furniture and art.

In a situation which sounds remarkably similar to the media blitz which Santa Fe was to experience in the 1980s, early visitors, especially those who earned their living writing, (John Galsworthy, Sherwood Anderson, H.L. Mencken, Mark Van Doren, Ezra Pound, Jack London, Sinclair Lewis, Paul Horgan and Carl Sandburg) couldn't resist telling readers of the town's appeal.

"…The countless writers who have been here and the scores who are here are pouring out a storm of what becomes publicity for Santa Fe—whatever form it takes, letters, magazine and newspaper articles, books—and the artists cause a lot of talk about Santa Fe," *The New Mexican* reported in May, 1926.

Like today, the attention which the town's remaining good looks inspire divides residents into the expansionists and the traditionalists. How to preserve the very charm which caused people to settle in Santa Fe in the first place against the heartbreaking changes which inevitably result with the arrival of thousands of passersby was and still is a two-edged sword which perpetually prevents the two camps from sinking into an apathetic state of complacency.

CONCERNED CITIZENS FORM
OLD SANTA FE ASSOCIATION

The Old Santa Fe Association was formed in 1926 by some of the literati, artists and other concerned Santa Feans. The general at the head of the army was author Mary Austin. The enemy was the Texas Federation of Women's Club which with the support of the Santa Fe Chamber of Commerce and business community wanted to establish a summer cultural center in Santa Fe. It was intended to be a kind of Chautauqua which would draw up to 3,000 visitors at a time. Since the year 'round population of Santa Fe at the time was only twice that number, it was an onslaught which locals felt they couldn't handle…or face.

According to *The New Mexican,* "…the line of demarcation between those striving to keep Santa Fe 'different' and those indifferent to what form the growth takes, is being more sharply drawn. But there is little doubt the farsighted policy will prevail and sentiment will be adequately organized to prevent losing Old Santa Fe in the rush of progress."

Sensing that the Santa Fe Anglo community was deeply split over the issue, the Texans realized that a tempest was brewing and called the entire proposal off.

Still, the publicity continued. In 1928, the Atchison, Topeka and Santa Fe Railway published a pamphlet entitled "They Know New Mexico: Intimate Sketches by Western Writers." Contributors included the omnipresent Mary Austin. Horrified to discover the name of the street she and her husband lived on was called Telephone Road in honor of the proud new telephone poles marching up the hill, she had a new campaign to wage.

Camino del Monte Sol, or the Road to the Sun Mountain, was what the Spanish had called the thoroughfare, Austin said, and it shouldn't be changed. The name went back to the original.

As for the group of poets, including Spud Johnson, Lynn Riggs, Witter Bynner and Daniel Long, which met at Austin's house, they called themselves the Rabelais Club, since they so frequently lapsed into a Rabelaisian mood. The Rabble was the way most people referred to them, however.

Founder of the Boy Scout movement in the U.S., author and naturalist Ernest Thompson Seton was another Santa Fe resident and one of Austin's frequent visitors.

Los Cincos Pintores, or the Five Painters, also lived on Camino del Monte Sol. Fremont Ellis, Willard Nash, Jozef Bakos, Will Shuster and Walter Mruk, who jokingly referred to themselves as "the five nuts in five mud huts," exhibited together frequently at the Art Museum. John Sloan, Carlos Vierra, Marsden Hartley, Gustave Baumann, Henry Balink and Randall Davey were also among the town's early artists, their medium being oil paint and watercolor.

Holding perpetual open house in his antique filled adobe house, a former water mill on Upper Canyon Road, Davey was one of Santa Fe's foremost bon vivants and outspoken devotees. "I wouldn't trade my life here where I can hunt, shoot, ride, for all the committee going and bootlicking you've got to do in a city for anything. An artist might starve for food here, but he'll starve spiritually in a place like New York," he said.

"My God! That such a place exists!" was the exclamation with which painter John Marin recorded his first reaction to Santa Fe. "It engulfs you. It's the best possible place to come alive. Space…it's unbounded. And that sky…it's a blank, empty wall…the most powerful emptiness I've ever known."

Legendary painter Georgia O'Keeffe would also be happily seduced by New Mexico. A 1929 houseguest of Mabel Dodge Lujan, a transplanted Easterner whose Taos salon was a kind of Southwestern Grand Central Station for many of the best known minds of the time, including D.H. and Frieda Lawrence, Max Eastman, Carl Jung, Leo Stein and Paul Strand, O'Keeffe recognized Mabel's need to dominate.

O'Keeffe quickly headed into the sunset to nearby Abiquiu, New Mexico, where she lived and painted most of her life. She would return to Santa Fe and a house on the Old Santa Fe Trail when she was well into her 90s. At the age of 98, she was given her first show at the New Mexico Museum of Fine Arts.

Some of Santa Fe's early painters were enticed to Santa Fe by the Museum of New Mexico. Able at that time to provide studio space, the museum also helped artists find living quarters, and even floated loans when necessary. The railroad was instrumental in another way to bring artists to the town. Aware that hanging Southwestern art in the stations stimulated business, company officials often traded tickets for canvases.

One of the early artists to make his home in Santa Fe, Carlos Vierra, also an architect, had a mission which transcended the power of the paint brush. "The deadly monotony of 10,000 American towns" was the way he referred to the rest of the United States from his vantage point in Santa Fe. Studying and photographing countless old buildings in the capital, he preached a sermon which architect John Gaw Meem would turn into "Santa Fe Style." The southwest had a rich architectural heritage which not only should be preserved, but carried on, Vierra insisted. His own adaptation was to be called the Spanish-Pueblo Revival style, a prime example being the Carlos Vierra House on the Old Pecos Trail.

Author Oliver La Farge whose novel *Laughing Boy* would be acclaimed an American classic was another Santa Fean who preached from the pulpit a sermon of preservation. "We can require that new buildings comply with certain style requirements," he proclaimed. "Fine. But pull out all the really old ones, everything that really backs up the city's claim to age, authenticity, and a special culture, and pretty soon it will look like a mouthful of false teeth, with a single old molar, the Governor's Palace, in one-corner. Nobody, but nobody, will cross the continent just to look at a well-constructed set of dentures."

Back in 1913, the Santa Fe Chamber of Commerce recognized the need to keep Santa Fe the way it was. Prizes were offered for houses which had flat roofs, were long and low rather than high and narrow, which were made out of adobe and which did not have bay windows.

A year later, the erection of the New Mexico State Exposition Building at the San Diego Exposition in 1914 became the model for the Museum of Fine Arts in Santa Fe, and helped to carry the message to the nation.

SANTA FE STYLE LAUNCHED IN 20'S

Architect John Gaw Meem was instrumental in bringing the crusade home to roost in Santa Fe. Designing his first "Santa Fe Style" houses by 1923, he was to leave his mark throughout the town. The Cristo Rey Church and the remodeling of the famed La Fonda hotel are among his numerous achievements appreciated and applauded during an era when America was waking up to the glory of native crafts.

Nowhere in the nation was there a greater opportunity to preserve the past than in New Mexico. Its Indian-Hispanic heritage seen in the pottery, silver, tinsmithing, embroidery, weaving and in what remained of the state's indigenous architecture with its *vigas, portals, corbels,* and *lattias* must not be allowed to be forgotten, early preservationists insisted.

The Spanish Colonial Arts Society and the Indian Arts Fund were founded in Santa Fe. The latter was, in fact, influential in triggering the Rockefeller Foundation to support the construction of the Laboratory of Anthropology in Santa Fe.

Earlier in 1880 the Archeological Institute of America, which had schools in Rome and Athens, had initially financed Adolph Bandelier's explorations of the Southwest. The results culminated in the Institute's decision to create a sub-unit based in Santa Fe to study American prehistory. Called the School of American Archeology, the new institution begun in 1907 would grow to become one of the nation's most important research centers of anthropology. In 1917, its name was changed to the School of American Research.

The Indian Arts Fund merged its collection of 6,000 examples of post-1850 Southwestern pottery, jewelry, textiles, costumes, basketry, and paintings with the newly created Laboratory of Anthropology in 1931. This collection draws scholars and crafters from throughout the world to its facilities hidden behind high adobe walls.

Mary Cabot Wheelwright, a transplanted Bostonian, was also instrumental in helping to promote Santa Fe as a major center of Southwestern studies. Her generosity provided the means to build the Museum of Navajo Ceremonial Art, renamed the Wheelwright Museum of the American Indian. Designed by William Penhallow Henderson, the building, in the shape of a Navajo ceremonial hogan, includes the Case Trading Post still in active use today.

Of all the early legendary names connected with Santa Fe, none is so well remembered by early transcontinental train travelers as Fred Harvey. Founder of the Harvey House chain of hotels and restaurants, the inveterate traveler's company was eventually to include Indian Detours, headquartered in the New Mexican capital. Harvey and his staff were astute enough to recognize that the public's growing fascination with the Southwest could turn a pretty penny.

English by birth, Harvey was appalled by the poor quality of food suffered by American train passengers in the late 19th century. Anxious to do something about the dilemma, he was granted the concession to run a string of restaurants called Harvey Houses, which quickly expanded into Harvey House Hotels, along the 12,000 miles of track traveled by the Atchison, Topeka & Santa Fe Railway.

Forced to stop their engines for refueling at least three times a day, railway officials figured they might as well do so at breakfast, lunch and dinner time. The engineer would feed the hungry engines, while Harvey could take care of the starved passengers.

It was a brilliant joint venture in which Harvey proved himself a phenomenal organizer and master head chef. Overnight, he was a household word.

Irish linen tablecloths, English silverware and superb food were trademarks of the 75 Santa Fe-style Harvey Houses in Kansas, Oklahoma, Texas, Colorado, Arizona, California, and New Mexico where service was provided by comely Harvey Girls.

A quick learner, Harvey was also fast to foresee the cash flow which could come from souvenir shops. He would again offer only the best in Indian and Hispanic art. Possessed with a discriminating eye, he began the operation but soon became too busy to continue traveling to the Indian reservations and pueblos to replenish the stores' stock.

The job fell to Herman Schweizer, who as early as 1899 was commissioning jewelry from Navajo silversmiths to sell in Harvey-owned curio shops, many of which were part of the hotels and/or restaurants.

Never one to waste a breath, Harvey is rumored to have died with the words "Don't cut the ham too thin" as his final order to his staff. The crown was immediately placed on his son's head, and Ford Harvey never missed a beat. The combination of hotel, restaurant and curio shop proved extraordinarily successful.

Before long almost all who traveled the Harvey House route were putting silver and turquoise jewelry, Indian pots and rugs and Hispanic *santos* in their suitcases to take home.

INDIAN DETOURS BRING VISITORS
TO SOUTHWEST

On May 15, 1926, a new angle on tourism in the Southwest opened up with the launching of Indian Detours set up by R. Hunter Clarkson, an employee of the Harvey Company. On that day, a Packard Eight touring car rumbled out of the Las Vegas, New Mexico railway station en route to Santa Fe via Glorieta Pass and then on to Albuquerque. Breaking their cross-country train journey for several days to see the pueblos and prehistoric ruins in the region, dudes from the East sat in the back seat. At the wheel was a driver who looked like

he'd stepped out of a Tom Mix movie. Sporting a ten gallon hat, a silk scarf, a colorful shirt, britches and high boots, the driver was accompanied by a Harvey courier. Young women, they too wore outfits which made them stand out at any corn dance. In fact, Harvey couriers inspired a fashion trend which the ladies of Santa Fe were quick to copy. It was a kind of up-market Navajo look. Sporting a soft cloche hat with the Indian Detours insignia on it, they wore brightly colored Indian inspired velveteen shirts and cotton skirts, sensible walking shoes, and turquoise and silver jewelry by the pound weight.

Blue jeans, concho belts, and boots by Tony Lama were to become the trademark of Santa Fe in the 1980s, with a good deal of help from designers Ralph Lauren and Calvin Klein.

Meanwhile, back in the 20s, a courier who didn't show up for work with squash blossom necklace, concho belt, and numerous bracelets was a courier without a job. Carefully chosen college-educated young women, couriers not only had to look the part of Southwestern pathfinders, but had to act the role as well.

Attending a school set up by the company, the women became conversant in anthropology, geology, history, and folklore. A fluency in foreign languages was helpful. And impeccable morals were mandatory.

Advertising the Indian Detours across the country, the company quickly expanded. Here was a way for visitors to see parts of the country which were inaccessible from the railway stations before fleets of touring cars, primarily Cadillacs, and buses began to meet the trains.

Although offered at first in northern New Mexico, the detours eventually expanded throughout the Southwest until the Depression eventually brought them to a close. By this time, America had come to realize what a jewel it possessed in Santa Fe.

No longer a Southwestern outpost but rather an increasingly sophisticated High Country holiday destination, the town was especially popular in the 30s and 40s during Fiesta. Begun in 1712 to commemorate the return of the Spanish to Santa Fe in 1692, the September event focuses attention on La Conquistadora. Taken with the fleeing Spanish and brought back with them on their triumphant return, this small statue is the patron saint of the state and a symbol of Hispanic unity.

Placed on the altar in a chapel within St. Francis Cathedral, the statue is a few minutes walk from La Fonda, Santa Fe's most noted hotel. The landmark building traces its origin to the first hotel on its site in the mid-17th century and is located on the Plaza at the end of the Santa Fe Trail.

Site of the Victory Ball after General Kearney conquered New Mexico in 1846 and headquarters of the Confederacy in 1862, the hotel, known as the Inn at the End of the Trail, later played host to General and Mrs. U.S. Grant, General William T. Sherman, and President and Mrs. Rutherford B. Hayes. Billy the Kid is even reputed to have washed dishes here.

The citizens of Santa Fe bought stock in a new hotel on the same popular street corner in 1920. Bought by the railroad, the hotel was leased to Fred Harvey whose company ran it from 1926 until 1969. John Gaw Meem was hired to transform the building's exterior into the popular Pueblo-style and Harvey's own outstanding collection of Indian, Hispanic and Mexican handicrafts were placed throughout lobby and public rooms.

What eventually became recognized as museum-worthy baskets, pots, blankets, church relics, and rugs served as a backdrop for afternoon tea at La Fonda and Sunday afternoon orchestra recitals.

The cover charge was 50 cents to dance the rumba, the foxtrot and the polka to Billy Palou's orchestra in the New Mexican Room. On special occasions, the baton was held by Xavier Cugat, Paul Whiteman and Lawrence Welk. The chef for 30 years was Konrad Allgaier whose skills continue to be praised by those who remember having their meals served in the Cantina by Harvey Girls in black dresses and huge white aprons.

Passing through a lobby full of Indians selling their necklaces and paintings en route to rooms full of Southwestern folk art and antiques, hotel clients quickly realized that to scores of Santa Feans, La Fonda was a second home.

"You were there at least once a day to meet your friends, have a meal, or simply to see who had come into town," says an old timer. "You heard every language, saw famous faces and caught up on all the gossip at La Fonda. Now that there are scores of hotels and restaurants, the lobby at La Fonda has ceased to be the melting pot it used to be. It was wonderful. God, how I miss it."

The good old days were to disappear forever with the outbreak of World War II. Santa Fe could not escape the consequences any more than the state of New Mexico could avoid becoming known as the location of the multi-colored, 40,000 foot high mushroom cloud which errupted over Trinity Site on July 16, 1945. The atomic bomb was introduced to the world on that day.

Scientists, en route to Los Alamos, New Mexico, where the bomb was developed, had been introduced to the state primarily via Santa Fe. "You would see them arrive from Albuquerque at the induction building on Palace Avenue. But you'd never see them leave. They did that by the back door," a third generation Santa Fean recalls. "They'd be whisked away secretly to nearby Los Alamos."

Robert Oppenheimer and Niels Bohr were among the many scientists at Los Alamos who would become famous for ushering in the atomic age. In the process, they integrated New Mexico into industrial and urban America.

CULTURAL MECCA: MUSIC AND ARTS ABOUND

Headlined the "Salzburg of the Southwest" by The New York Times, Santa Fe would gain an image in the next half century as one of the nation's cultural meccas. With only two art galleries and two restaurants listed in the telephone book in 1946, the ranks of both would swell to well over a hundred by the mid 1980s. Over one million visitors a year from across America now join the town's 53,000 year 'round inhabitants to shop, eat and pay homage to Santa Fe's museums. "The art of the craftsman is a bond between the peoples of the world." These words by founder Florence Dibell Bartlett appear over the entrance to the Museum of International Folk Art, which has become reason alone for many visitors to come to town.

The Alexander Girard collection with its 10,000 pieces of folk art on display (over 106,000 pieces remain in storage) occupies a wing especially designed to house it. Wide-eyed children and adults come for an hour, remain half a day, and vow to return for a week.

Cleverly though tightly displayed, the Girard collection ranges from Mexican ceramic figures to Japanese aerospace toys. A noted architect and designer, Alexander Girard inherited the core of the collection from his father. Adding to it and eventually filling 4,000 cardboard boxes, the pair offered their naive treasures to the museum, which accepted them joyfully.

Having pursued "things made without the assistance of modern technology," Girard insists that folk art "isn't a subject really. It's a hodge-podge." The museum reflects this viewpoint. Iroquois beadwork, Moroccan toy motorcycles, English juvenile paper theaters, Victorian doll houses, Staffordshire earthenware figures, and Italian marionettes are all on view.

To listen to many of the world's finest singers and musicians who perform in Santa Fe each summer is yet another reason to visit this cultural mecca.

The Santa Fe Chamber Music Festival fills the seats in the St. Francis Auditorium at the Museum of Fine Arts. The Desert Chorale draws attendance at the Santuario de Guadalupe. The Orchestra of Santa Fe performs at the Lensic Theatre, the Santa Fe Symphony at the Sweeney Center, and the Ensemble of Santa Fe at the Loretto Chapel. British American Theater fills the seats of the Greer Garson Theater named after the Oscar-award winning actress who lives in nearby Pecos. While at the Santa Fe Opera, the lights of neighboring Los Alamos lend the illusion of Nagasaki to a performance of Madame Butterfly. Perched high on a hill with Albuquerque to the south and the Rockies to the north and east, the opera building, because of its dramatic, sweeping lines, presents an aeronautical look. It is "a great desert bird poised for flight. But its adobe-colored walls are reassuringly terrestial," according to critic James Idema.

The creation of John Crosby, the opera began modestly in 1956 with a 450-seat capacity. Fire destroyed the original building, but relentless fund-raising has kept the opera alive from its inception and has helped to pay for the award-winning current building which opened in 1968.

A magnet which draws opera lovers from across the nation to hear such well known performers as Frederica Von Stade, Rosalind Elias, Ashely Putnam, Sherril Milnes and Judith Blegen, the opera is also a highly desirable summer proving ground for 40 apprentice singers. They are personally chosen by Crosby from over 700 applicants.

Finishing their last mouthful of chocolate mousse at a tailgate picnic in the parking lot, swallowing a final sip of champagne in the Opera Club, polishing off the last bite of apple pie at Furr's cafeteria, ticket holders scurry to be in their seats by 9 p.m.

Baton in hand, Crosby may very well be in the pit to lead the orchestra and the singers through *Elektra, The English Cat, Traviata, The Magic Flute,* or *Lulu.* If it rains, many in the uncovered section get wet. Almost everyone will slip on a sweater. And if the moon is out, no one will need a flashlight to find his car when it comes time to drive home.

In increasing numbers, the rich and the famous have bought houses in Santa Fe. Many have done so in part because of modest state taxes and an ability to maintain a low New Mexican profile. They want to be inconspicuous and are able to do so. Like scores of other Santa Feans, they wear the "school uniform"—blue jeans and boots, a sartorial disguise which makes it possible not to stand out in a crowd.

It's important to appear friendly in Santa Fe. Therefore the well-known often list their names and numbers in the phone book. But try to find out their street addresses! Peoples' whereabouts are some of the city's best kept secrets.

Restaurants are good places in Santa Fe to find out who is in town. Landmarks are the Pink Adobe, El Nido, Josie's, the Shed, and the Compound. Scores of others open and close before they make the telephone book. With the proliferation of restaurants, finding a place to eat in Santa Fe, especially for Northern New Mexican cuisine, is easy.

It's getting to someone's house for a barbeque or cocktail party that offers the challenge. Only 46 of the county's 236 roads have signs to mark them. Many of them are dirt. Unpaved roads in the middle of town aren't uncommon. "Go past the piñon, turn left at the juniper, keep right at the 7-11 and look for the bashed-in mailbox. That's us." Thoughtful hosts tie ribbons to their telephone poles, bandanas to their barbed wire and fly custom-designed flags from their gateposts. Anything to let guests know they've arrived.

S.O.S. MEANS "SAVE OUR SANTA FE"

The biggest question in town is, Do Santa Feans want Santa Fe to have arrived? Each newcomer wants to be the last to have crossed the drawbridge before it is raised. "Aspenization," or the proliferation of countless boutiques, condos, hotels, and fast food stands is the battle cry which unsheathes the swords of diehard conservationists. "S.O.S.," they holler, having formed the Save Our Santa Fe Association to do something about it.

Yes, buildings in the downtown are restricted to Territorial- or Pueblo-style architecture, and are restricted in height, they say. But what about the fake adobe and barely recognizable conformity to standards? What about the neon signs, hamburger stands, and countless motels on the fringes of town? What about the proliferation of boutiques and souvenir shops downtown forcing out the stores where one's grandparents and parents used to shop? What about the increase in traffic? Is anybody paying attention to the changes? Is anybody heeding the facts?

With a beginning average price tag of $250,000 on a house or condominium out of reach of most wage-earning residents, the town's skyrocketing real estate market is of major concern to civic leaders. They realize the cost of housing is devastating to Santa Fe's Hispanics who comprise 64 per cent of the capital's population and 23 per cent of whom fall below the poverty level.

"We have a housing crisis," says Jarratt Applewhite who heads the city's Task Force on Affordable Housing. Members feel $30,000 to $60,000, at least in the 1980s, spells affordable. "We have a slogan, 'Where are our children going to live?'" he says. "People come up to me and say, 'Children, hell! Where are *we* going to live?'"

Living is really what Santa Fe is about, newcomers are quick to recognize. "I was burned out. I'd put in my years earning and saving for retirement. Yet, I didn't have anything I was truly looking forward to," a three year resident of Santa Fe tells friends who notice a new birth in the older man. "I moved here and for the first time in years, I feel truly alive. What happened? A major reason is the sky. I am never, never tired of watching the clouds shift, change color, swoop, glide, and finally sail right over the tops of the mountains. I feel it isn't exaggerating to say that Santa Fe has saved my life."

SPIRITUAL SEEKERS AND HEALERS ABOUND

The city's location, said to be above one of the earth's major centers of magnetic force, is frequently spoken of as an explanation for Santa Fe's age old attraction for people anxious to tune out the old and tune into the universe's more "meaningful" messages. Its protection from the supposedly upcoming world apocalypse by a cone of spiritual grace is also spoken of by the city's numerous soul searchers as reason enough to move here.

Faith healers, philosophers, religious leaders, psychics, and clairvoyants all abound in the City Different. Newspapers are full of their ads. Acupuncturists, reflexologists, cranial balancers, Ayurvedic physicians, aura readers. Whatever you want, Santa Fe has it.

The annual Health and Fitness Expo gives believers a chance to attend seminars given by some of the nation's leading proponents of alternatives to mainstream medicine. Speakers have included Joseph Cohen on "Crystal Healing;" Dale Figtree on "The Cleansing and Detoxification Diet: A Process of Deep Healing;" Ingrid Naiman on "Stress in the Horoscope;" Gurudas on "Flower Essences, Gem Elixers and Vibrational Healing"; and David Christopher on "Be Your Own Herbalist: Maybe Someone Else's."

Psychics in Santa Fe have their day in the sun, too. At the Psychic Fair, scores of psychics of varying persuasions sit behind their crystal balls, tarot cards, and Visa cards. Salesmen are also there to sell self-hypnotic tapes to rid people of acne, addictions and other nasty negativisms.

Followers of the philospher Gurdjieff, Zen Buddhists and Tibetans can also be found in Santa Fe. Local gossip would have it that the latter arrived unannounced one day at the home of one wide-eyed David Padura. The message was straight forward. "We have come from Tibet," they said. "We have been instructed to find a place between the mountain of the sun and the mountain of the moon where we are to build a 'chorten' underground and spin our prayer wheels. And that place is your backyard."

A community of Hindu Sikhs also lives near the New Mexican capital. Aware that one must create his own employment in a community where unemployment is chronic, they recognized the town's need for security guards and quickly cornered the market. Dressed in khaki uniforms and white turbans, Sikhs often patrol the aisles and check shopping bags at many of Santa Fe's leading supermarkets and dime stores.

Quality of life is Santa Fe's greatest asset. It is the major reason people want to come here, *Megatrends* author John Naisbitt told City Fathers anxious to expand Santa Fe's economic base. Forget big industry, Naisbitt counseled. There is barely enough water for the city as it is now. Tourism is what the city should focus on.

Visitors are mesmerized by Santa Fe's extraordinary landscapes. They are intoxicated by the glorious weather. They return home raving about her culture, the outdoor activities, including skiing in winter and hiking in summer. Concentrate on improving Santa Fe's attraction by preserving and improving what the city can already best provide, tourism experts insist.

There is horse racing at The Downs. There are countless special events including Spanish Arts & Craft weekend and Indian Market.

Colleges include St. John's, a branch of the Annapolis, Maryland, institution with its Great Books curriculum, the College of Santa Fe, the Community College of Santa Fe, and the Northern New Mexico Community College.

SUSHI, TUMBLEWEED AND SUNSETS

There are sushi bars, gourmet food shops, private caterers, chocolatiers offering bon-bons flown in from Belgium, and magazine stands selling French and Italian publications. There are rodeos, tumbleweed in the barbed wire, strands of red chili hanging beside front doors, pungent piñon smoke from thousands of fireplaces.

Like a perpetual benediction, a light pure and clear washes the city clean every morning. Like a Broadway encore, a blazing sunset tucks her into bed every night. The sound of applause reverberates off countless adobe walls as citizens turn from the departure of the Sun God in the west to the arrival of the Moon Goddess in the east. Her Ladies in Waiting—Mars, Jupiter, Venus: they, too, begin to strut down a runway illuminated by a thousand footlights.

The air is cool. A soft, silky breeze brings the distant howl of a coyote. Los Angeles is 95. Dallas is 100. New York has 75 per cent humidity. Houston has 92. Santa Fe has none and and the thermometer will drop to 55 by morning.

Santa Fe has been discovered, then forgotten. Rediscovered, then reforgotten. One minute she's center stage, the next she's back in the wings. "Santa Fe: Is the Magic Gone?" asks *Metropolitan Home.* "Will Desert Chic Spoil Old Santa Fe?" queries *U.S. News & World Report.*

It is a query which has been circulating in the New Mexican capital for decades. Chances are it always will. The absence of a major airport, the lack of water, the abundance of Indian land surrounding the city—these circumstances

fortunately work against an endless Santa Fe real-estate boom.

In the early 1980s, the media blitz brought thousands of newcomers to the city. Real estate prices soared. The catered cocktail party had arrived. By the late 1980s, the spotlight had shifted. Tourism returned to normal. The price of houses fell a little. A reasonable calm returned to the land.

The truth is that Santa Fe has a very special appeal. There are no boardwalks here and cotton candy. Instead, there are *portals* and *piñon* candy from Señor Murphy. There aren't big resorts, yet. There are historic hotels and guest ranches. There are no waves to play in, no beaches to lie on. There are mountains to climb, horses to ride, and the Rio Grande to go rafting on.

Santa Fe is High Country. It is a land of blazing sunsets, pungent *piñons* and shooting stars. *Figaro* is at the opera. The coyotes are in the hills. There was a recent $10,000 reward for information leading to the arrest of the robbers at the Ortiz Gold Mine. It's $2 to watch the polo matches on Sunday afternoons.

"The chi-chi bird has landed with talons of silver and beak of gold. All is lost." The words were scribbled on the wall of a restaurant's men's room. Customers were eating sirloin. Outside, low riders were circling the Plaza. Waitressess were serving margaritas. At the Governor's Palace, Indians were selling jewelry. Customers were asking for their checks. In the barrio, residents were facing their bills.

Sugar coated, Santa Fe is not. It is a living city, a sanctuary for those seeking higher thinking, a poor place to look for a job. "Santa Fe is where your karma hits the fan" is the way a contemporary newcomer put it.

"Be there a Paradise on earth; it is this, oh, it is this, oh, it is this!" author Carolyn Bancroft gushed in the 30s, referring to an ancient Persian inscription. Then, she added, "When my visit ended, I went away reluctantly. But, I was already planning a return—and another—and another. With steady repetition, I tasted the atmosphere of Santa Fe."

Eventually, she, too, experienced enlightenment. "...Today, I can blithely remark...that 'things are seldom what they seem; skimmed milk often masquerades as cream," she saw. "Now I enjoy Santa Fe for what it is, not as a Paradise."

Legendary settlement at the end of the trail, Santa Fe enjoys being known as the City Different. For many of her admirers, the city is truly the start of something new.

Santa Fe Scene

There is something for everyone on the Santa Fe scene. Museums and churches, shopping or eating, exploring back streets, gallery hopping, listening to a concert, enjoying a craft fair: whatever one's druthers, there's a way to be satisfied.

You'll wait 30 minutes to get a seat at the Shed for blue corn tortillas. Even longer at Josie's for tamales and apricot pie. Huevos rancheros and home fries at Pasqual's are on early morning minds. Tried and true restaurants in Santa Fe are in demand. But their popularity requires patience.

Summer trade is normally good, especially for the Indians under the portal at the Palace of the Governors, constructed in 1610 by Governor Pedro de Peralta. For decades, Indians have come into town from their pueblos to lay out their turquoise and silver jewelry by 8 a.m. In the 60s, when Anglo crafters invaded their turf, the Museum of New Mexico solved the problem. The Indians were part of the museum's exhibition, officials said. The white man wasn't.

True to its Spanish heritage, Santa Fe is a city of churches. Many are among the finest examples of early adobe in the nation, including the 18th century Santuario de Guadalupe and San Miguel Chapel. The Cristo Rey Church, built in 1940 to commemorate the 400th anniversary of Coronado's exploration of the Southwest, is a classic example of New Mexican mission architecture of the Spanish period. It contains a great stone *reredos,* or altar screen, considered the most superb Spanish colonial work of ecclesiastical art created in New Mexico.

Perhaps no building in Santa Fe draws more visitors than the Museum of International Folk Art. Admirers of Southwestern art flock to the Museum of Fine Arts, whose collection of 19th and 20th century New Mexican art contains works by O'Keeffe, Ufer, Sharpe, Henri, Gaspard, Davey, and Balink. The building's architectural origins stem from New Mexico's building at the San Diego Exposition of 1914. Called the Cathedral of the Desert, it was inspired by the mission churches at the San Felipe, Acoma and Cochiti pueblos. It was so successful that the state decided to duplicate it in Santa Fe as the Museum of Fine Arts.

Considered as much a landmark as any of the city's plaqued buildings, the Hotel La Fonda stands on a site where there has been a hotel since the middle of the 17th century. Designed in Spanish-Pueblo style, the current 1920 building was owned by the Atchison, Topeka & Santa Fe Railway and was leased to the Fred Harvey Company in the 1920s. Indians sold their wares in the lobby. Dudes and cowboys, European aristocrats, local characters and ranch hands drank at the bar. Tea was served in the afternoon. Big bands played at night.

The hotel haunts the memories of those who recall the good old days. "Years ago, when you said 'downtown,' you meant La Fonda," says one of the city's old timers. "You went there to see friends, hear gossip, learn who new had rolled into town. There wasn't any place else to go."

For visitors today, downtown Santa Fe is a shopper's and gallery hopper's paradise. With new shops opening all the time, one can be kept busy for days poking and exploring Sena Plaza, Canyon Road and Galisteo St.

Downtown Santa Fe is quiet most nights. People are usually home by ten. But there are those who linger. Go down Burro Alley, pass by the Palace of the Governors, cross the Plaza, and you'll probably bump into Don Diego de Vargas, Zapata y Lujan, Ponce de Leon, Kit Carson, Billy the Kid, and Archbishop Lamy. They are often out for a stroll in the full moon.

The Girard Foundation of the Museum of International Folk Art houses over 106,000 objects from around the world donated by designer-collector Alexander Girard. The folk art aficionado is like a kid in a candy shop in the colorful and imaginatively displayed exhibition hall designed by Mr. Girard.

Pages 36–37

The La Fonda Hotel is the Inn at the End of the Trail. Just off the Plaza, the original hotel dates from the middle of the 17th century.

Left: During the 1930s, 40s and 50s, the La Fonda lobby was a crossroads for local intellectuals, artists, eccentrics, and Indians peddling jewelery. A few old timers still linger in the lobby.

Above: The courtyard of the Museum of Fine Arts.

The Pink Adobe restaurant on the Old Santa Trail is typical
of Santa Fe architecture. The exterior stucco coat of adobe
buildings comes in many subtle hues; pink, ochre, chocolate,
beige, even sage green.

Canyon Road is well known for galleries and shops, and is a popular walking street for visitors.

Below: The turquoise portal on Palace Avenue shades the entrance to Sena Plaza and other quality shops.

During July and August, renown artists perform at the Santa Fe Opera (above) and at the Santa Fe Chamber Music Festival (left) which is held at the Museum of Fine Arts.

*The Gross-Kelley Company building was one of the first
examples of Spanish-Pueblo Revival architecture. Today, it
houses several artists' studios.*

Left: Top of the facade of the Lensic Theatre, a Santa Fe landmark since 1930.

Above: "The Oldest House" is an 18th century building allegedly on the site of a 13th century Indian pueblo. It is tucked away on East De Vargas Street.

Pages 50–51

The Hispanic culture is celebrated throughout Santa Fe in public wall art and in private homes.

Mi querido pueblo Nuevo Mejico.
Al que tal parece que nació
...para Sufrir...
Y ser explotado por nativos,
crillios, amigos y enemigos.

Al que tal parece estar sentenciado
a tener escaso de lo abundante que
—su territorio da.
Al que, también puede pensar,
hacer y decir; llorar y reir.

Landscapes

Interstate 25 North from Albuquerque is the fast way to Santa Fe. For first time viewers of Southwestern landscape, the hour long drive is a true epiphany. The piñon and juniper dotted tawny terrain spreads away for miles—flat for awhile, then undulating, popping up with extinct volcanic cinder cones. Finally, off on the horizon, mountains loom into view.

On blowy days, tumbleweed tears across the highway, snagging in car fenders, or getting trapped in a barbed wire fence on the other side.

Stand on a mesa, climb a mountain, drive down a dirt road in landlocked New Mexico—it's landscapes and skyscapes that dazzle you. In the fifth largest state in the union, there are over 122,000 acres of breathtaking open spaces. Backdropped by an ever-changing sky, highlighted with wild asters, sunflowers, piñons, junipers, spruce, and chamisa, land is New Mexico's most appreciated asset.

Fewer than two million residents leave a lot of room for nature to perform in. Snowcapped peaks up to 13,000 feet; grasslands as plush as green velvet; canyons cut deep by the Rio Grande River bordered by blossoming fruit orchards; arroyos littered with cattle bones and beer cans, waiting to become rushing riverbeds after a heavy thunderstorm; whispering mountainsides of ponderosas shafted by sunlight and carpeted with pine needles: the New Mexican landscape surrounding Santa Fe constantly changes.

Land of Enchantment is on every license plate. It's easy to understand why. Take that still talked about summer evening when the clouds back of the Sangre de Cristo Mountains put on an eye dazzling performance that brought the city to a reverential standstill. It began with an overture of seething, monumental, shifting marshmallow cloud banks. Imaginations took flight as pastel pachyderms in sherbet colored tutus danced a slow motion ballet. The standing ovation was for the ten minutes of lightning bolts in the belly of the whale. To the ancients, the entire experience would have been an omen. To Santa Feans, it was yet another of nature's infinite extravaganzas.

Blessed by beauty, Santa Feans stop their cars to watch a triple rainbow and raise their glasses at cocktail parties to stunning sunsets.

Artists have been drawn to the New Mexican landscape for generations. Stuart Davis even complained about it. "You always have to look at it," he said. Marsden Hartley recognized immediately that New Mexico "is not a country of light on things. It is a country of things in light."

Writer D. H. Lawrence never got over his years here. "For a greatness of beauty I have never experienced anything like New Mexico," he wrote. "…It (has) a spendid silent terror, and a vast far-and-wide magnificence which (takes) it way beyond mere aesthetic appreciation. Never is the light more pure and overweening than (here), arching with a royalty almost cruel over the hollow, uptilted world…so beautiful, God! so beautiful…Ah, yes, in New Mexico the heart is sacrificed to the sun and the human being is left stark, heartless, but undoubtedly religious."

Photographer Ansel Adams caught the magic as well. "The skies and land are so enormous and the detail so precise and exquisite," he exclaimed. "…Wherever you are, you are isolated in a glowing world between the macro and the micro—where everything is sidewise under you and over you, and the clocks stopped long ago."

Of all the artists associated with New Mexican landscape, Georgia O'Keeffe is the fastest to come to mind. Never to return East, O'Keeffe told the rest of the world why. "If you ever go to New Mexico, it will itch you the rest of your life."

Rainbow watching is a popular pastime for Santa Feans. Here, the spectrum arches over La Tierra, a subdivision.

South of Santa Fe off I-25, the wide flat vistas are punctuated with piñon covered volcanic cinder cones and outlined by far reaching mountain ranges.

Pages 56–57

Black Mesa, a sacred site on the San Ildefonso Pueblo is framed by an Appaloosa. Originally an Indian breed, Appaloosa horses are a popular part of the New Mexico landscape.

Pages 58–61

The soul of Santa Fe is in the sky. From dawn to dusk, awe-struck drivers stop cars to gaze as turbulent cumulus clouds billow through the blue, abstract anvil shapes emerge over mountains, and sunsets silhouette mesas.

The landscape around Abiquiu and Ghost Ranch northwest of Santa Fe was the subject of many of Georgia O'Keeffe's paintings.

The Atchison, Topeka & Santa Fe Railway still operates as a freight train around Northern New Mexico.

Santa Fe is surrounded by Indian archeological sites such as Bandelier National Monument (left), and petroglyphs (above), or rock carvings, hidden away in the Galisteo Basin and in the Rio Grande River valley.

Lilacs to Snowflakes

Double rainbows, bolts of lightning, blazing sunsets, black, red and purple sunsets, pink and grey sunsets, snowflakes on piñons, hailstorms in July, sunbathing in December, cauldrons of clouds, tidal waves of clouds, flotillas of clouds, emerald skies, flamingo skies, steel gray skies, raindrops on tin roofs, moonlight on adobe walls, sunshine on chamisa, wind through ponderosas, breeze through junipers, sunflowers in August, geese in formation in winter, hummingbirds in the hollyhocks in summer.

Santa Fe is a city of seasons. It is a 7,000-foot-high settlement where spring, summer, fall, and winter take turns coming in the front door and going out the back. Santa Fe has over 300 days of sunshine a year. In winter, subzero temperatures often climb into the cozy 50s and 60s. Come dusk, the air is pungent with the fragrance of piñon smoke from thousands of fireplaces.

Summer days are pleasantly warm, but you'll pull on a sweater at night. Twenty five percent humidity and the locals are griping. March and April, the wind and mud are infuriating. Lilacs in May make the city celestial.

June is the hottest month. It is the beginning of summer thunderstorms. In fall, aspen trees flutter their gold leaves like flocks of canaries in the sunshine. Tumbleweed jams up in the barbed wire fences. Pine cones lie still in the forests.

New Mexico covers 121,000 square miles of diverse terrain. It plunges through six of the seven life zones, from tundra to the lower Sonoran desert. Santa Fe is "High Country" where snow storms come down from Colorado and tail ends of hurricanes pass over the border from Mexico.

Shooting stars streak through the night. Cumulus clouds as big as nations, tiny clouds as skittish as mice take turns passing on parade throughout the day. Rainstorms bring out the perfume of piñon. Dry spells crack the earth like spatterware.

Christmas is a magic season. Snow is on the mountain tops. Chili ristras as red as entrails hang under *portals*. Woven reed wreaths festooned with dried flowers hang on turquoise doors.

Farolitos by the hundreds, nay, by the thousands sit like miniature Humpty Dumptys on adobe walls, outline alleyways, flank streets, and guard rooftops. Paper bags full of sand, they have fat white candles inside their bellies.

There are bonfires at crossroads. Hot chocolate in kitchens. *Posole,* hominy and pork stew. *Biscochitos,* anise-sugar cookies. And most of all, *Las Posadas.*

For nine consecutive nights before Christmas, Santa Feans eagerly await knocks on their doors. Finally it comes, along with the singing of *peregrinos,* pilgrims. It is an ancient tune, one that goes back to the 16th century settling of New Mexico. *De larga jornada,* (From a very long journey,) *Rendidos llegamos,* (very weary are we,) *Y así imploramos,* (and come to implore you) *Para descansar.* (for shelter.) It is the re-enactment of Mary and Joseph's search for shelter on the night of Jesus' birth.

Pueblos perform Christmas dances. The *Matachines* date to the Moors who introduced it to the Spanish who introduced it to the Indians.

There's a gentleness, a comfortable companionship about Santa Fe's seasons. From lilacs to snowflakes, from Brother Sun to Sister Moon, the grandeur and the glory is divided into four spellbinding acts: spring, summer, fall, winter. Days become months, months become seasons, seasons become years. In New Mexico, Mother Nature has a special regional repertoire.

At Christmas, candlelite paper bags, or farolitos, *festoon the adobe walls and rooftops of Santa Fe. These painted* farolitos *were designed by Nona Wesley, and the regional wreath was designed by Anne Forbes.*

Pages 70–77

Santa Fe's four seasons come as a surprise to many. Lilacs in the spring; summer thunderstorms and sun tea; golden aspen and cottonwood trees in fall; and snow fit for skiing provide year round variety.

Indian Market

"We're going to Indian Market." "We went to Indian Market." "We missed Indian Market." Held annually the third weekend of August, this two-day event is considered by close to 100,000 viewers and buyers to be a primary reason to come to Santa Fe. At no other place in the United States are so many Native American artisans assembled with their creations, all of which have been screened for authenticity and quality, all of which can be bought.

Friday night, the Plaza is blocked off. Carpenters erect 350 booths. Exhibitors, mainly from the Southwest, unload their pots, jewelry, beadwork and paintings. By eight a.m. Saturday, most of the award winning art has been purchased by collectors and dealers.

The public spotlight hasn't always shone so brightly on Indian art, however. There was even a time when Indians themselves were sufficiently unconscious of their own rich artistic heritage that they switched to producing souvenir items for tourist shops. Rose Dougan and Vera von Blumenthal saw the problem as early as 1917 and convinced potters at San Ildefonso pueblo north of Santa Fe to maintain their standards. Financed by a $2,000 endowment from Dougan, funds were generated to be given as prize money in an annual pottery competition. It was thought correctly that competition would encourage Indian craftspeople to maintain quality.

The first annual Southwest Indian Fair and Industrial Arts and Crafts Exhibition was held in 1922 in conjunction with the 210th Santa Fe Festival. Curators today look back in awe at the items offered for sale at these early marketplaces. Dakota Sioux brought priceless heirloom beadwork, Apache and Navajos brought basketry and weaving not seen before in public.

Among the early prize winners was a young woman from San Ildefonso who would put contemporary pots on the list of top collectibles. Her name was Maria Martinez. Over the next half century, her black-on-black pots would be sought by museums and collectors worldwide.

Under the administration of the Southwest Association on Indian Affairs and recognized as a way Indians could supplement incomes, Indian Market is now so popular that over 400 artists submit over 1,400 entries to the judges. By 6 a.m. on Saturday, competitors start taking their entries and ribbons out of the Judging Room at La Fonda and back across the Plaza to their booths. The buying has begun!

In 1985, an unknown first time participant, Joyce Growing Thunder Fogarty, an Assiniboin from Rim Rock, Arizona, walked off with Best of Show. She had dazzled judges with a man's beaded ceremonial outfit. Fogarty's courage in coming to Indian Market, in fact, broke a longstanding tradition. For many years, jewelry and pottery had enjoyed primary status as the bedrock of contemporary Indian arts, including Cochiti black-on-cream storage jars, traditional Hopi kachina dolls, Pima coiled tray baskets, Santa Clara black wedding jars, and incised and painted pots from San Juan Pueblo.

Among the regular exhibitors at Indian Market are celebrated potter and octogenarian Margaret Tafoya. She is frequently in a booth near Helen Cordero, credited with launching the boom in ceramic Story Teller dolls.

Says Lee Cohen, owner of Gallery 10, "Indian Market is a marvelous opportunity to see and evaluate the new rising stars. It is definitely the time for trendsetters to start setting their trends."

Sculptor Bob Haozous applauds a growing movement by Native Americans to bring their art up with the times. "Art is what you are today, not what people wanted it to be 100 years ago. You can't see through your grandfather's eyes. Use history as a reference point," he tells young Indian artists. "Then observe yourself." Indeed, each year, younger artists break from the traditional.

In August, the annual Indian Market held on the Plaza attracts Native American craftspeople and collectors from around the country.

Left: Mary Owens, a Navajo from Arizona, is an award winning weaver. All categories of crafts are judged, and winning works are usually the first to be sold.

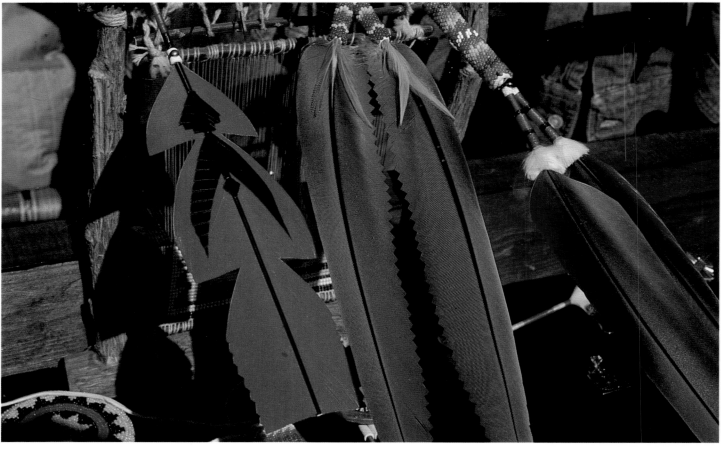

Behind Adobe Walls

For the visitor to Santa Fe, one of the town's great mysteries is what lies behind the beautiful organic adobe walls that flank the narrow streets. Camino del Monte Sol, Acequia Madre, El Caminito, Camino de Cruz Blanca; are we in Spain, Portugal, Mexico or the United States?

Indeed, the atmosphere of the City Different is truly foreign, with Santa Feans guarding their privacy behind adobe walls. Once inside private houses, one encounters the unique regional "Santa Fe Style." As applied to architecture, interior design and the decorative arts, Santa Fe style originated in the first half of the 20th century. During the 20s, 30s, and 40s, Santa Fe was discovered by Easterners—artists, intellectuals and members of the old guard—who brought their individuality, their freedom of expression and frequently the family antiques, with them.

Establishing homes, the newcomers found that European antiques fit beautifully into the cozy adobe setting. Soon they discovered the regional symbols: Navajo weavings; Indian pottery; kachina dolls; beaded moccasins; Spanish colonial tin sconces; church crosses; colorful *santos*, or carved wooden religious figures; and spectacular carved wooden doors. These Southwestern artifacts and crafts were successfully incorporated with European antiques. A Rio Grande blanket or Acoma pot established a sense of place in private houses while adding eyecatching accents of color and design.

The eclectic Santa Fe look had nothing to do with interior designers, or any self-conscious attempt to create a stylized living environment. It was the result of people of heritage, security, sophistication, and flair who, like expatriates, had traveled with their personal belongings and "settled" in the "new world" of the American Southwest.

Today, there are, of course, some superb regional interiors. But few vintage Santa Fe interiors survive, reflecting eclectic design freedom. Neither do most new home owners attempt to emulate the cross-continental look. Rarely accompanied by family antiques, newcomers frequently rely on interior designers and regional craftsmen to create for them the so-called "Santa Fe Style." The result is an increasing number of interiors with the same pale palette in fabrics; contemporary Southwestern paintings in primary colors; teeth baring folk art coyotes and bears; writhing wooden snakes; Indian drum coffee tables; and *equipale* chairs. The "Oh, so Santa Fe" style has, in fact, been canned and promoted nationwide by interior design publications.

Getting as much press as Santa Fe interiors is the city's current architectural style, an adaptation from traditional to solar. In the 1920s, the two men most instrumental in establishing and preserving the Spanish-Pueblo Revival style were artist Carlos Vierra and architect John Gaw Meem. They rallied influential people to establish tough architectural style ordinances for new construction, and encouraged faithful preservation of historic buildings. The Greek Revival and Victorian periods were rapidly eclipsed by the enthusiastic support for the Spanish-Pueblo Revival style.

Today, the architectural style ordinances hold loose rein on new construction in historic downtown Santa Fe. Outside the bounds of governmental control, the piñon covered hills around Santa Fe are a battleground for contemporary architectural vernaculars as the traditional Pueblo-style gives way to solar and semi-solar adobe houses. With very few successful attempts to wed classical architectural vernaculars with the technological constraints of solar construction, and the unlimited design potential of adobe, a city full of insular architects has produced a landscape of houses as canned as their interiors.

Given its anthropological, archeological, mystical, spiritual, artistic, colonial, and tri-cultural heritage—nowhere in the United States is there such unlimited potential for individual style in architecture and interior design as there is in Santa Fe, the City Different.

Pages 84, 86-87

Architect Nat Owings, former partner of Skidmore, Owings & Merrill, designed this ranch in the 1960's. A personal interpretation combining pueblo and territorial styles, the ranch, when lived in by the Owingses, effectively evoked an earlier day in its furnishings and atmosphere.

The interiors of the Santa Fe second home can be effectively furnished without holding up a gold mine. The main ingredients here are white and light.

Potter Pricilla Hoback, represented by the Fenn Gallery, entertains guests at her ranch with earthy goose egg place settings. Napkins and place mats are woven by Sarah McCook, represented by La Mesa.

Living with collections is popular in Santa Fe. The display for a santos collection (Left) was designed by Alexander Girard. Navajo weavings and bead work (Top) greet visitors entering a condo designed by Betty Stewart. Chinese ivories (Bottom) are unexpectedly at home in a charming Mexican cabinet.

96-97

Eclectic freedom is hard to find in contemporary Santa Fe interiors. With its English antiques, Italian lamps, European inspired tile floor and Navajo Eye Dazzler rugs, this living room is one of the most stunning in the Southwest.

Inspired by his South American travels and by the aesthetic potential of adobe, arthitect/interior designer/ painter Ron Robles gives fresh form to a house for Mel Fillini.

100-101

Artist Ringsella Pingselli does commissions for both public and private clients. Here, she enlivens the Shed Restaurant with a sense of color and whimsy.

Artist Ford Ruthling incorporates his paintings, collage doors and metal work designs with just about every South-western symbol in one of Santa Fe's most charming and fanciful houses.

Creators

Estimated to gross $50 million a year in art sales, the third highest volume in the nation after New York City and Los Angeles, Santa Fe is home to over 1,400 creators including painters, sculptors, ceramists, architects, weavers, woodcarvers, writers, composers, potters, jewelers, and photographers. The spectrum of talent in Santa Fe is vast.

Many artists are represented by over 125 local galleries. The boom in gallery sales is a recent phenomenon, however. Until the 1920s, Santa Fe hosted numerous trading posts. It was there that traders and collectors, Anglos for the most part, bought Hispanic folk art and Indian crafts. The first truly commercial galleries opened in the late 1950s. They sought to ride the wave of public interest in Western and regional art, and continue to do so.

Today, art in Santa Fe is not confined to strictly regional traditional themes. The Center for Contemporary Arts provides a comprehensive program for the exhibition, making and study of the contemporary arts. Many expand the definition of regionalism. Others aren't derivative of Southwestern art at all.

Also on the contemporary frontier is Shidoni, one of the nation's foremost foundries. With eight and a half acres of sculpture gardens, Shidoni represents over 70 sculptors who work in all media.

In an effort to bring significant cross fertilization to the insular Santa Fe art scene, the Santa Fe Institute of Fine Art attracts Richard Deibenkorn, Helen Frankenthaler, Paul Jenkins, Larry Bell, Nancy Graves, and Nathan Olivera, who conduct workshops for artists attending from around the country.

Many other well known creators live in and around Santa Fe or have second homes in the area. They include sculptor Bruce Nauman, playwright John Simon, actor and producer Robert Redford, sculptor Juan Hamilton, composer Morton Subotnick, painter Agnes Martin, composer Roger Miller, author Edward T. Hall, composer Deuter, painter Clark Hulings, painter Fritz Scholder, and poet Scott Momaday.

What is it that has drawn creators to Santa Fe and the surrounding area for decades? They explain it best themselves. D. H. Lawrence wrote, "The moment I saw the brilliant, proud morning shine up over the deserts of Santa Fe, something stood still in my soul, and I started to attend."

Santa Fe fan Calvin Klein is under the spell as well. "It's the colors, the light, the sky, the richness of the earth...There's a purity that exists there, which is the essence of my style," he said.

Noted travel writer Jan Morris enthused, "Nothing could ever discountenance the physical splendors of Santa Fe...No environment I know seems more unmistakably to guarantee the sublime permanence of things."

Painter John Martin rationalized that "the country is so damned big—that if you succeed in expressing a little—one ought to be satisfied and proceed to pat oneself."

Of course, Georgia O'Keeffe was mesmerized by the peculiar hard, white, bright light. She made the mysteries of the Southwestern light and landscape famous in her paintings. Writer Mabel Dodge Luhan, instrumental in bringing O'Keeffe to New Mexico, described the effect it had on the artist. "Take an exquisite, sensitive mortal like Georgia O'Keeffe... and suddenly lift her from sea level to the higher vibration of a place such as (New Mexico) and you will have the extraordinary picture of her making whoopee."

Armond Lara, painter

Left: David Anderson, sculptor
Above: Woody Gwyn, painter
Below: Judy Chicago, multimedia artist
Over leaf: John Fincher, painter

Left: Katherine Sylvan, weaver
Above: Celia Rumsey, painter
Below: J. Boles, weaver
Over leaf: Tavlos, sculptor

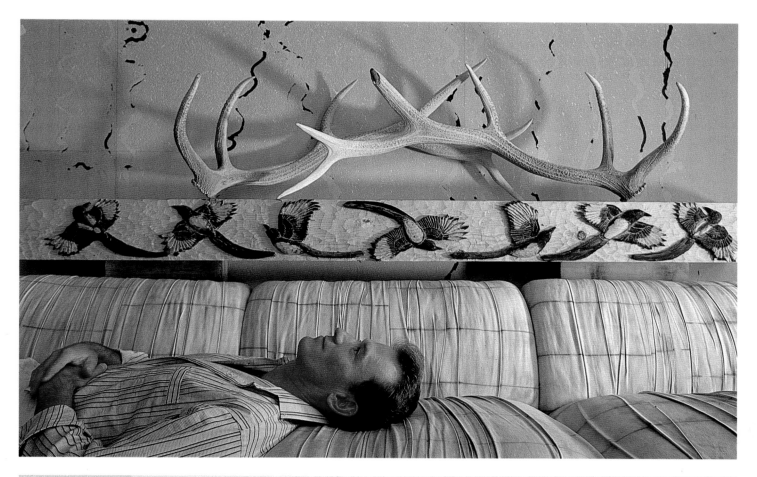

Gail Rieke, collagist & Zachariah Rieke, painter (left)

Above: David Parsons, woodcarver
Below: Ben Ortega, woodcarver

Richard Davila, woodcarver

Left: Rick Dillingham, ceramist
Above: Teresa Archuleta-Segal, weaver
Below: Charles Greeley, painter & Bunny Tobias, ceramist

Left: Randy Lee White, painter
Above: Jesus Bautista Moroles, sculptor
Over leaf: Amado Peña, painter

Left: Paul Sarkisian, painter
Above: Constance De Jong, sculptor

Left: Joan Meyers, photographer
Above: Ruben Romero, composer & classical guitarist.
Below: Bill Martin, electronic music composer
Over leaf: Bernique Longley, painter

Above: Aline Porter, painter & Eliot Porter, photographer
Below: R. C. Gorman, painter

Above: Betty Stewart, architect
Below: Slim Green, saddlemaker
Over leaf: Walter Cooper, painter

Holy Adobe

The Spanish came to New Mexico expecting to find great mineral wealth. They were disappointed to find thousands of Pueblo Indians instead. Switch gears, said the Crown. Let your riches be spiritual: Convert the natives. To this end, the Spanish government promoted extensive missionary activity.

Churches must be built. In addition to their Bibles, early Franciscans traveled north from Mexico City to remote New Mexico with a standard "building kit." It contained axes and spades, nails and hinges. In 16th century New Mexico, one started from the ground up, literally.

Adobe, or earth mixed with straw and water, was the way the Indians built their pueblos for centuries. Warm in winter, cool in summer, it was practical. More important to the friars, the earth was there to be had. New Mexico was an outpost. It took six months for a wagon train to get from Mexico City to Santa Fe. Construction materials weren't strapped to the donkeys' backs. If you lived in New Mexico, you made do. For the clergy, holy adobe answered their architectural prayers.

Designer, engineer, foreman, building inspector, the brothers taught the Indians to make bricks from the adobe. The missionaries knew the simpler the design, the faster the construction. No vaulted ceiling. No stone work. Minimal fenestration. Sculptural elegance made up for early mission churches' stark simplicity, both at the pueblos and in Santa Fe. Indian potters knew the wonders of clay. Ancestral skill translated to the refinement of churches, the design of which remained predominantly the same in New Mexico from the 17th century until the middle of the 19th century. During this time, missionaries directed the construction of over 80 churches. In remote areas where the brotherhood didn't penetrate, the Penitentes, rural societies of the deeply religious, built *moradas,* or private chapels. A few remain today.

Santeros, makers of religious images, who painted *retablos,* pictures, and fashioned *bultos,* statues, were in heavy demand during the Spanish colonial era. They catered to parishioners' love for ornamentation. *Reredos,* or brightly painted altar screens depicting Biblical tales, were popular in colonial New Mexico where bright colors were limited to sunsets and story telling to firesides.

With the exception of the Palace of the Governors in Santa Fe, significant 17th and 18th century Spanish architecture in New Mexico is found in a few churches in and around the capital. The Holy Cross Parish at Santa Cruz de la Canada, 1733; San Jose de Gracia at Las Trampas, 1760; and the Santuario de Chimayo, 1816, are in the nearby countryside. The San Miguel Chapel, 1610, the "Oldest Church;" the Santuario de Guadalupe, 1776; and the contemporary El Cristo Rey are in town.

Today, restoration is going on inside many churches. More important, preservation is beginning on those whose massive adobe walls are eroding. Freezing and drying without constant repair makes adobe bricks expand, contract and crumble. Citizens' committees, the Archdiocese of Santa Fe, the state's Historic Preservation Division—numerous organizations are putting their shoulders to the task.

A legacy of extraordinary beauty and charm, the churches of New Mexico are a part of America's rich and diverse architectural heritage. For Santa Feans and visitors alike, holy adobe has an emotional and aesthetic appeal that is a special regional experience.

The Holy Cross Parish at Santa Cruz near Española was built in 1733, forty three years before Thomas Jefferson signed the Declaration of Independence.

Pages 136–137

In many Northern New Mexican churches, the reredos, or painted wood altarscreen, is a fine example of primitive Spanish Colonial religious art. The reredos at the Holy Cross Parish Church at Santa Cruz (p. 136) and at the Santuario de Chimayo (p. 137) have been beautifully restored.

Above: Las Golondrinas is a Spanish Colonial village museum in La Cienega south of Santa Fe. In front of the chapel are two beehive shaped horno, or bread ovens which were brought to the new world by the Spanish.

Pages 140–141

Archbishop Lamy's Chapel at Bishop's Lodge (left) and the Loretto Chapel (right), the First Gothic style building west of the Mississippi and completed in 1878 aspire to European architectural standards.

The Santa Fe Cathedral of Saint Francis of Assisi (upper left) begun by Archbishop Lamy and completed in 1886. Most other religious buildings in and around Santa Fe are older charming colonial adobe structures. They include San Jose de Gracie at Las Trampas circa, 1760 (lower left); the Santuario de Chimayo, 1816 (upper right); and the penitente morada at Las Golondrinas (lower right).

Pages 144–145
The church of the Sacred Heart in Nambe is seen through a coyote fence, the stakes of which are driven deep into the ground to prevent the critters from digging underneath.

The massive adobe walls of the Holy Cross Parish at Santa Cruz ner Española are an impressive architectural feat. On the more quaint side are Nostra Señora de Los Remedios,

Galisteo (upper left); the chapel on the Morning Star Ranch, Alcalde (upper right); Saint Miguel Chapel, Santa Fe (lower left); and the Santuario de Guadaloupe, Santa Fe (lower right).

Religious culture around Santa Fe is evident in colorful graveyards; the miraculous circular stairs in the Loretto Chapel; the votive candles and crutches testifying to the heal-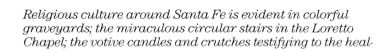*ing power of the "Holy Mud" at the Santuario de Chimayo; and the candlestand at the Santuario de Guadaloupe.*

Indian Dances

Check the newspaper, call the Pueblo Governor's office, ask at the Santa Fe Chamber of Commerce. It takes homework to know when the Indians are dancing at the eight pueblos around Santa Fe. Sometimes scheduled, always spontaneous, rarely on Bulova watch time, lines of bouncing dancers suddenly appear. The beat of the drums, the pounding of hundreds of moccasin clad-feet on a parched plaza: the ceremony begins, unrehearsed, unpolished and uncontaminated by contemporary rhythm or movement.

The Indian dance is a prayer, performed with reverence. It is also a dramatic representation. It can include pantomine, sometimes humor, but always the solemnity of a mass. David danced before the Lord. Pueblo Indians dance to the gods to help the seasons along, to promote the fertility of plants and animals, to encourage rain, to ensure a good hunting season. Man must be in harmony with the universe. Dancing helps to pave the way.

Some dances are the culminating performances of rites which have been going on for days—purification, retreats, sacred ceremonies. Others honor patron saints introduced to the pueblos by the Spanish in the hope of reducing the gods to a God.

Corn dances are frequently held. They relate to the germination, maturation, and harvesting of the crop. Rain dances are important. So are animal dances: the buffalo, the butterfly, the deer, the antelope, the eagle. Basket dances symbolize food which preserves life. Christmas dances honor the Christ child. Easter the risen Lord. A mingling of faith. A cross fertilization of cultures.

A prayer-meal in the house, holy water in the church, prayer-sticks before a shrine, rosaries before the saints. Indian dances and ceremonies aren't to be judged. They are to be treasured and enjoyed.

A student at the University of New Mexico, a dentist in Roswell, a guard at Los Alamos, an office worker in Santa Fe: wherever you are, whatever you do—if you are a Pueblo Indian, you return home at least once a year for a dance. In traditional dress, you are back with the family. For the men, spruce twigs symbolize longevity. Gourd and shell rattles imitate the swish of summer rain. Feathers and tufts of cotton are clouds and sky. Women's headdresses, or *tablitas,* represent sun and moon.

Colors have meaning. Blue is for sky, green is vegetation, yellow is pollen, red is for life blood. Death comes in black.

Suddenly, it is over. Just as they appear to have no beginning, Indian dances seem to have no ending. They start and stop as unexpectedly as a shooting star. A swig of Coke, a bite of fry bread, a chat with a friend: the dancers are milling around.

Is the magic over? Will they dance again? In ten minutes? In an hour? Indian time! No one knows. Wait patiently and they will begin again.

Spectators come and go with picnic lunches. Children watch from daddies' shoulders. Octogenarian Indians seek shade under colorful umbrellas. They are proud of grandchildren's fancy footwork. Crafters sell turquoise and silver jewelry, pots and beautifully beaded moccasins. Indeed, many pueblo dances open to the public are harmonious days of cultural appreciation.

During Indian dances and feast days, traditional dress is worn. Especially beautiful are the women's headresses, or tablitas. They are carved, painted boards with designs representing the sky, clouds, sun, moon, and other motifs of sacred significance.

Overleaf: At the Santa Clara feast day, pueblo children enjoy the dances from the top of the kiva, a meeting house for special governmental and ceremonial matters.

Pages 156-157
The color and spectacle of the feast day dress.

Pages 158-159
Onlookers enjoy the Santa Clara feast day dances while drummers set the tone.

Viva La Fiesta

Zozobra, De Vargas, La Reina and La Conquistadora share equal billing at the annual Fiesta de Santa Fe every September. A three day blend of history, religion and merrymaking, the city's Hispanics look on the event as a commemoration of their New Mexican heritage. Anglos see it as a fine time to enjoy fireworks, effigy burning, parades and mariachi bands. As for local Native Americans, they diplomatically avoid reopening old wounds.

The oldest community celebration in America, Fiesta honors the reconquest of the city from Pueblo Indians by General Don Diego de Vargas. Taking command of a regiment of 200 Spanish colonists who had fled to El Paso from Santa Fe after their defeat in the Pueblo Revolt, De Vargas and his men re-entered the city on September 12, 1692. Cutting off the Indians' supply of water, the Spaniards were quickly in command. By 1694, over 1000 settlers and their families were back living around the plaza.

The budget for the first Santa Fe Fiesta held in 1712 under the direction of Lt. Gov. Juan Paez Hurtado was 55 pesos and an unspecified amount of beeswax. The money paid for a priest to give a sermon relating to the event, vespers, a Mass and a procession. The beeswax was for candles to be used in the religious events.

Fiesta didn't catch on immediately, however. It wasn't until 1919 when the governor of New Mexico, Octaviano Larrazolo, made an official proclamation reviving the event that Fiesta became an annual celebration. From the ranks of the city's Hispanic families, De Vargas and his men, Los Caballeros, La Reina, the Fiesta Queen and her court are chosen each year by the Fiesta Council. The 17th century soldiers and the 20th century royalty fill their Fiesta days with parades, balls and public appearances. For many, the Desfilo de los Niños, or children's costume and pet parade, as well as the Historical/Hysterical Parade, are highlights of the weekend.

Our Lady of the Rosary, or *La Conquistadora,* maintains a more solemn posture. Her role is to focus attention on the religious significance of Fiesta. Legend says that De Vargas prayed to the Madonna, the most sacred statue the fleeing colonists took with them after the Indian revolt. If she would grant him a re-conquest, he would build her a chapel and honor her with a feast day. Things happened as prayed, even though 70 Indian warriors were put to the sword and 400 women and children enslaved. Today, La Conquistadora emerges from her chapel in the cathedral each Fiesta for a procession.

The real star of the three day weekend is Zozobra, a 42 foot, ugly-faced marionette also known as El Rey de los Diablos, or more commonly, Old Man Gloom. First appearing at Fiesta in Santa Fe in 1926, the effigy was designed by artist Will Shuster. Its roots were the belief of primitive people that evil spirits must be purged from the world.

On the Friday night of Fiesta weekend, over 30,000 frolicking spectators pay to enter Fort Marcy Park to watch the enormous thick-lipped, hawk-nosed, pop-eyed, papier maché Zozobra go up in flames. Sponsored by the Kiwanis Club, the "burning" is a highly successful scholarship fund event.

One minute, two minutes—the longer it takes Old Man Gloom to become memory, the happier the crowd. Zozobra groans and moans as spectators scream, "Burn him, burn him!" As sour-faced Zozobra disappears in a blaze, euphoric Santa Feans and visitors welcome the return of La Fiesta.

The highlight of the Fiesta is the burning of Zozobra, or Old Man Gloom. The Furries dance away the evil spirits (left) just before Zozobra is set ablaze (overleaf).

Pages 162–163

A floatload of giggly Hispanic girls enlivens the Historical/Hysterical Parade.

Pages 164–165

José Morfin as Don Diego de Vargas, the Spanish conquistador who re-conquered Santa Fe in 1692, and Bernadette Ortega as La Reina are the stars of the Fiesta.

Pages 168–169

The Historical/Hysterical Parade passes by the Palace of the Governors (above) and crowds gather for the burning of Zozobra (below).

Local Color

Perhaps the most "foreign" place in the United States in terms of culture and lifestyle, Santa Fe has a feeling, a texture and a color scheme all her own. She shows her "colors" in many ways. Sometimes, they are vibrant. More often, they are traditional.

Local color extends beyond the palette, however. It includes lifestyle. Santa Fe calls herself the City Different. She lives up to the name. She can be flashy and self-consciously eccentric. Or, she can be refined and sublime—even the epitome of unself-conscious style.

Architecturally, Santa Fe leans on her past. In the historic downtown, citizens outraged by a commercial building boom painted "WAKE UP" on construction barriers. They did so with turquoise and silver spray paint, however.

Neon is verboten. Shop signs are discreet. Old guard galleries and trading posts knock the boots off first-time visitors with wall-to-wall inventories of eyedazzler Navajo rugs, pots and Indian jewelry. Glitzy new "faux adobe" shops with imported goods from "abroad," suspiciously L.A. in look, appall old guard Santa Feans.

One of the most traditional aspects of Santa Fe, and the quality which gives the place its true local color, is the fact it is still a down and dirty town emerging from the earth. Historically unpretentious, Santa Fe is on the brink of being tarted up, however. The craft of authentic organic adobe construction is giving way to cost-conscious commercial buildings.

Real adobe is the essential texture of Santa Fe. A mixture of earth, straw and water, it comes in many hues: beige, gray, ochre, chocolate, and pink. Windows are trimmed in blues and greens. Beautiful carved wooden front doors come up from Juarez or are made by local wood carvers. Santa Fe doors along charming side streets are focal points of local color.

Vintage pickup trucks are parked along narrow side streets. Matching malamutes wearing bandanas ride in the back. Low riders circle the Plaza, unadorned and downright shabby with neglect. To outsiders, the Plaza is tacky. To locals, it's "so what, it's Santa Fe"—worn down with indifference, wrinkled with age.

Dress like an Indian, be taken for a cowboy, pile on the turquoise and silver jewelry, wear blue jeans to the opening night of the Santa Fe Opera, black tie and boots to a gallery opening. Local color definitely includes clothing. Whatever you wear, it's laissez faire.

Local color is ubiquitous on culturally inspired public wall art all over town. Motifs include the Spanish arriving in Santa Fe, the Virgin Mary, Acoma pots, pueblo scenes, snakes, and the zia sun symbol.

And of course, Santa Fe has its local colorful characters. Members of the younger generation, many of whom are trying on new lifestyles and sincerely seeking higher mindedness, will eventually take over the roles of the few revered old timers who remain. The City Different is truly a haven for individuality and diverse lifestyles and tastes. Mutual respect and tolerance is Santa Fe's prized and protected social heritage.

Local color in Santa Fe lingers in memory long after one has left. It never ceases to impress those fortunate enough to remain. Still foreign, very regional, its particular palette combines the colors of an atmosphere and attitude of a very special place. "I am dying to live in Santa Fe!" How many times does one hear this?

Santa Fe—"Fanta Se!" For some it is a reality. Santa Fe has chosen them. For many, it remains a dream to come true in another incarnation.

The zia sun symbol on a building on Cerrillos Road is an Indian-inspired motif.

Page 173

A Santa Fean strolls along West San Francisco Street in a town where style and individuality in everyday dress is taken for granted.

Pages 174-175

Feathers worn in men's hair at Indian dances or special events symbolize the glowing zenith. Lisl's hat has no such spiritual significance.

Pages 176-177

Vigas, or structural beams, cast shadows on adobe walls. Decorative corbels, or carved wooden capitals, support many of Santa Fe's portals.

Pages 178-179

Fanciful florettess are on a wall behind a bench.

Pages 182-183

The Case Trading Post at the Wheelwright Museum of the American Indian is styled after a real Navajo trading post and operates in the traditional consignment fashion. The Santo Domingo pot is by Robert Tenorio and the weavings are Navajo.

Pages 184-185

Cigar store Indians and cowboys at the Tin-Nee-Ann Trading Company on Cerrillos Road watch traffic on one of Santa Fe's main commercial strips.

Pages 186-187

Every summer renowned flamenco dancer Maria Benitez hypnotizes audiences with her swirling performances (left). Another "you've got to see it to believe it" is "Very Cherry," (right), a 1963 Chevy Impala low rider owned by David Leyba, a founding member of the Limited Edition Car Club of Santa Fe.

Pages 188-189

At Shidoni (left), a sculpture by Ali Baudoin is seen through a work by Ed Haddaway. These contemporary pieces are contrasted by the traditional color and texture of a blanket and stucco wall (right).

Pages 190-191

Las Golonodrinas, a Spanish Colonial village museum in La Cienega offers an opportunity to learn the history and feel the texture of period buildings.

Saddle Blankets
The
OLDEST
INDIAN
and
MEXICAN
TRADING
POST
In The
UNITED
STATES
Navajo

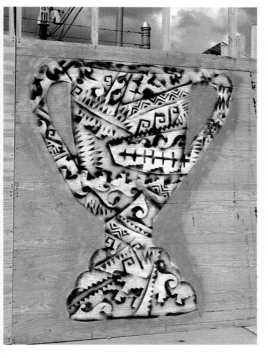

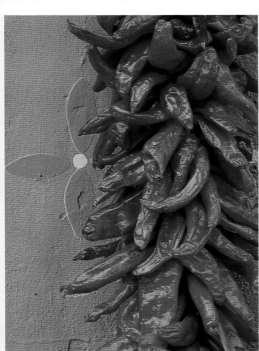

© 1987 Herring Press Inc.

Produced by Jerry and Sandy Herring
Published in 1987 by Herring Press, Inc.,
Houston, Texas. All rights reserved. No part of
the contents of this book may be reproduced
without the written permission of the publisher.
All individual photographs are the copyright of
Lisl Dennis. Dust jacket photograph of Lisl and
Landt Dennis by Nancy Brown.

Typesetting by
Characters, Inc.
Printed in Japan

First Printing 1987
Second Printing 1987
Third Printing 1989

Library of Congress
Number 87-80841
ISBN 0-917001-06-0

Published by
Herring Press, Inc.
1216 Hawthorne
Houston, Texas 77006
(713) 526-1250

Distributed by
Texas Monthly Press
P.O. Box 1569
Austin, Texas 78767
(512) 476-7085